MotoGP™ 2024 RIDERS' WORLD CHAMPION

MotoGP™ 2024 CONSTRUCTORS' WORLD CHAMPION

MotoGP™ 2024 TEAMS' WORLD CHAMPION

SBK™ 2024 MANUFACTURERS' WORLD CHAMPION

SBK™ 2024 TEAMS' WORLD CHAMPION

WorldSSP 2024 RIDERS' WORLD CHAMPION

WorldSSP 2024 MANUFACTURERS' WORLD CHAMPION

DUCATI CORSE

2024 Official Yearbook

MARIANNA
1956

2024, il Sistema Ducati si dimostra davvero efficace.

Scrivere la lettera di apertura per questo libro sta diventando davvero una dolce abitudine.
In questa edizione dell'Official Yearbook Ducati Corse si trovano raccolte tutte le immagini più significative di un'altra stagione sportiva strabiliante per Ducati, che concludiamo aggiungendo alla nostra bacheca sette nuovi Titoli Mondiali ottenuti tra MotoGP, WorldSBK e WorldSSP.

Dopo la gioia pazzesca del 2022 e le "vittorie della consapevolezza" del 2023, per questo 2024 è giunto il momento di celebrare l'efficacia del "Sistema Ducati". Un sistema che si ispira agli insegnamenti di Galileo Galilei, il padre della scienza moderna, che ci ha portato a essere i migliori nelle competizioni in pista, e che applichiamo anche nella progettazione, nel design e nello sviluppo del prodotto di serie, portando fieramente l'ingegneria Made in Italy in tutto il mondo. Come ci ha insegnato Galilei, infatti, il metodo Ducati si fonda sull'integrazione tra ragionamenti matematici, teoria ed esperimenti che devono dimostrare la correttezza della teoria.

È anche attraverso l'applicazione di questo metodo che in MotoGP siamo arrivati a esprimere un'evidente superiorità tecnica con i "Fantastici 4" piloti Ducati, il neo Campione del Mondo Jorge Martín insieme a Francesco Bagnaia, Marc Márquez ed Enea Bastianini, a occupare le prime quattro posizioni della classifica generale. La nostra stagione 2024 è davvero stata incredibile: diciannove gare su venti sono state vinte da una moto Ducati!

In questo scenario di dominio delle tecnologie "made in Borgo Panigale", Jorge Martín e Pecco Bagnaia hanno fatto la differenza, mettendo in scena un duello per il Titolo ancora più equilibrato di quello dell'anno precedente. Pecco ha vinto più gare, ma Jorge è stato più costante e alla fine è lui il Campione quest'anno. Si tratta del quarto Titolo Mondiale MotoGP per la nostra Azienda, dopo quelli di Stoner nel 2007 e di Bagnaia nel 2022 e 2023. È una vittoria che dimostra come le storie d'amore possano anche concludersi con uno stupendo finale, e fatico a pensare a un modo migliore per celebrare il lavoro svolto in questi anni insieme a Jorge e al team Pramac Racing.

Anche nel Mondiale Superbike abbiamo mantenuto il nostro indiscusso ruolo da protagonisti, nonostante il cambio dei regolamenti e il livello sempre più alto dei Campionati. In WorldSSP abbiamo confermato con Adrián Huertas e il team Aruba.it Racing WSSP il Titolo Mondiale per il secondo anno consecutivo, mentre la Panigale V2 si è confermata la miglior moto in griglia portandoci al terzo Titolo Mondiale Costruttori della nostra storia. In WorldSBK ci è mancata la vittoria della classifica generale, ma i nostri piloti ufficiali Nicolò Bulega e Álvaro Bautista (Aruba.it Racing - Ducati) sono saliti sul podio finale e grazie alle loro prestazioni e alla qualità della Panigale V4 R, capace di portare alla vittoria ben sei piloti diversi quest'anno, abbiamo conquistato il ventesimo Titolo Costruttori Superbike della nostra storia: un traguardo straordinario nel più importante campionato riservato alle moto derivate di serie.

Il 2024 è stato anche l'anno del debutto per la divisione Off-Road di Ducati Corse, la cui prima stagione si è conclusa subito con un Titolo, con Alessandro Lupino che in sella alla Desmo450 MX ha vinto il Campionato Italiano MX1. È un successo che conferma la validità del progetto, nato per sviluppare una gamma completa di moto e motori Ducati per il fuoristrada specialistico, che ora proseguirà con la partecipazione al Mondiale MXGP 2025, l'arrivo nelle concessionarie della moto per i nostri appassionati clienti e le prime prove del modello 250cc.

Abbiamo inoltre concluso con soddisfazione la seconda stagione da fornitore unico del FIM Enel MotoE World Championship con un costante miglioramento dei riferimenti cronometrici, in media di oltre mezzo secondo più veloci rispetto a quelli registrati nel corso del 2023.

Ovviamente, i trionfi nel mondo racing non sarebbero possibili senza l'impegno quotidiano di tutte le ragazze e i ragazzi che, a Borgo Panigale e nelle filiali di tutto il mondo, lavorano per sviluppare prodotti straordinari, belli, tecnologici e performanti, realizzandoli con cura e qualità e raccontandoli con storie ed eventi emozionanti, in linea con la nostra mission di regalare ai Ducatisti esperienze memorabili grazie a moto oggetto di una magica combinazione di tecnologia sofisticata e bellezza sensuale, in un inconfondibile stile sportivo italiano.

Se dovessi scegliere un momento per descrivere la qualità straordinaria di questo 2024 riporterei tutti quanti al World Ducati Week e alla sensazione magica nel vedere la "marea rossa" affollare il Circuito di Misano nell'edizione più grande di sempre. È in quel contesto che si è materializzata l'essenza della filosofia Ducati, animata dal continuo scambio di competenze e informazioni tra il mondo delle competizioni e quello del prodotto di serie. Abbiamo presentato al mondo la nuovissima Panigale V4 e qualche ora dopo l'abbiamo messa nelle mani degli eroi che ci regalano emozioni ogni weekend sui circuiti di tutto il mondo, con un risultato strabiliante in termini di prestazioni e di spettacolo.

Stile, performance, qualità, passione, sportività, tecnologia, bellezza, sportività. Essere Ducatisti significa vivere quotidianamente tutte queste emozioni e, in un momento storico in cui il Sistema Ducati è vincente nel mondo, è un orgoglio sempre più grande.

2024, the Ducati System proves to be effective.

Writing the opening letter for this book is really becoming a nice habit.
This edition of the Ducati Corse Official Yearbook contains all the most significant images of another amazing sporting season for Ducati, which we conclude by adding to our showcase seven new World Titles obtained between MotoGP, WorldSBK and WorldSSP.

After the crazy joy of 2022 and the 'victories of awareness' of 2023, for this 2024 the time has come to celebrate the effectiveness of the "Ducati System". A system that is inspired by the teachings of Galileo Galilei, the father of modern science, which has led us to be the best in track racing competitions, and which we also apply in the research, design and development of our products, proudly bringing Made in Italy engineering all over the world. As Galileo taught us, the Ducati method is based on the integration of mathematical reasoning, theory, and experiments that must demonstrate the correctness of the theory.

It is through the application of this method that in MotoGP we have come to express an evident technical superiority with the "Fantastic 4" Ducati riders, the new World Champion Jorge Martín together with Francesco Bagnaia, Marc Márquez and Enea Bastianini, occupying the first four positions in the general classification. Our 2024 season has truly been incredible: 19 out of 20 races were won by a Ducati motorcycle!

In this scenario of domination of "made in Borgo Panigale" technology, Jorge Martín and Pecco Bagnaia made all the difference, staging a duel for the Title even more balanced than the previous year. Pecco won more races, but Jorge was more consistent and in the end he is the Champion this year. This is the fourth MotoGP World Title for our Company, after Stoner in 2007 and Bagnaia in 2022 and 2023. It is a victory that shows how love stories can also end with a wonderful finale, and I struggle to think of a better way to celebrate the work done in these years together with Jorge and Pramac Racing.

We have also maintained our undisputed role as protagonists in World Superbike, despite the change in regulations and the increasingly high level of the Championship. In WorldSSP we have confirmed the World Title for the second consecutive year with Adrián Huertas and the Aruba.it Racing WSSP team, while the Panigale V2 has again proved to be the best bike on the grid, taking us to the third Manufacturers' World Title in our history. In WorldSBK we missed out on the overall championship win, but our official riders Nicolò Bulega and Álvaro Bautista (Aruba.it Racing - Ducati) reached the final podium and thanks to their performance and the quality of the Panigale V4 R, capable of taking six different riders to victory this year, we won the twentieth Superbike Manufacturers' Title in our history: an extraordinary achievement in the most important Championship reserved for production-derived motorcycles.

2024 was also the year of the debut for the Off-Road division of Ducati Corse, whose first season ended immediately with a Title, with Alessandro Lupino who, riding the Desmo450 MX, won the Italian MX1 Championship. This success confirms the effectiveness of the project, created to develop a complete range of Ducati motorcycles and engines for specialist off-roading, which will now continue with participation in the 2025 MXGP World Championship, the arrival of the bike in dealerships for our passionate clients and the first tests of the 250cc model.

We also concluded with satisfaction the second season as sole supplier of the FIM Enel MotoE World Championship with a constant improvement in the lap times, on average more than half a second faster than those recorded during 2023.

Obviously the triumphs in the racing world would not be possible without the daily commitment of all the men and women who, in Bologna and in branches around the world, work to develop extraordinary, beautiful, technological and high-performance products, creating them with care and quality and telling them with exciting stories and events, in line with our mission to give Ducatisti memorable experiences delivered by high end motorcycles made of a magical combination of sophisticated technology and sensual beauty, in an unmistakable sporty Italian style.

If I had to choose a moment to describe the extraordinary quality of this 2024 I would take everyone back to the World Ducati Week and the magical feeling of seeing the 'red tide' crowd the Misano World Circuit in the largest edition ever. It is in that context that the essence of the Ducati philosophy materialized, animated by the continuous exchange of expertise and information between the world of racing competition and that of series product. We presented the brand-new Panigale V4 to the world and a few hours later we put it in the hands of the heroes who give us emotions every weekend on circuits all over the world, with an astonishing result in terms of performance and spectacle.

Style, performance, quality, passion, technology, beauty, sportiness. Being a Ducatisti means experiencing all these emotions on a daily basis and, in a historical moment in which the Ducati System is a winner in the world, it is an ever greater source of pride.

Claudio Domenicali
CEO Ducati Motor Holding S.p.A.

DUCATI
CORSE

Per il terzo anno consecutivo, il Campione del Mondo MotoGP è un pilota Ducati!

Dopo i Mondiali vinti da Francesco Bagnaia nel 2022 e nel 2023, quest'anno è stato Jorge Martín a scrivere un'importante pagina nella storia del motociclismo, in sella alla Desmosedici GP del team Pramac Racing. Nel 2024, che ha visto Ducati imporsi ancora una volta con numeri da record, Jorge e Pecco hanno regalato emozioni straordinarie agli appassionati. Questi due piloti eccezionali hanno dato il massimo per contendersi il titolo fino all'ultima gara, alzando continuamente il livello della competizione per dimostrare chi fosse il migliore. Hanno messo in risalto non solo il loro straordinario talento, ma anche uno stile, una filosofia, un metodo di lavoro, uno spirito di squadra e un modo di vincere che rappresentano il cuore pulsante di Ducati Corse.

Alla fine, è stato Martín a conquistare l'Iride, coronando il suo sogno di diventare Campione, tenendo testa a uno strepitoso Bagnaia in grado di mettere a segno ben undici successi in questa stagione. Oltre a Bagnaia e Martín, Marc Márquez (Gresini Racing MotoGP) ed Enea Bastianini hanno entusiasmato tutti i Ducatisti, lottando fino all'ultimo per il terzo gradino del podio mondiale.

Un applauso, quindi, ai nostri Fantastici 4, gli artefici delle diciannove vittorie ottenute da Ducati in questa stagione. Un record assoluto non solo per noi, ma anche per la MotoGP, con una Desmosedici GP che è salita sul gradino più alto del podio in tutte le gare del calendario 2024, eccetto una. Quest'anno abbiamo raggiunto traguardi storici e significativi, come la centesima vittoria nella classe regina, arrivata nella gara di casa a Misano, nel cuore della Motor Valley, grazie a Enea Bastianini nel GP dell'Emilia-Romagna. Solo una settimana dopo, in Indonesia, abbiamo celebrato la nostra centesima pole position in MotoGP, con un totale di sedici pole ottenute da Ducati quest'anno.

Il 2024 è stato un anno davvero da incorniciare: la nostra migliore stagione di sempre nella classe regina, impreziosita dalla vittoria del nostro sesto titolo costruttori (il quinto consecutivo) e del titolo mondiale Team con la squadra ufficiale, il Ducati Lenovo Team.
Ancora una volta, abbiamo confermato la forza del nostro progetto, grazie anche all'impegno e allo spirito di squadra dei nostri otto piloti e dei quattro team satellite: Francesco Bagnaia ed Enea Bastianini; Jorge Martín e Franco Morbidelli (Pramac Racing); Marc e Alex Márquez (Gresini Racing MotoGP); Marco Bezzecchi e Fabio Di Giannantonio (VR46 Racing Team). Un grazie speciale a tutti loro per averci permesso di crescere e raggiungere questi straordinari traguardi.

Il Mondiale MotoGP corona una stagione sportiva eccezionale, in cui abbiamo conquistato anche il titolo Costruttori e Team in Superbike con i piloti ufficiali del Team Aruba.it – Racing Ducati, Nicolò Bulega e Álvaro Bautista, rispettivamente secondo e terzo sul podio del Mondiale. Abbiamo inoltre conquistato il titolo Piloti e Costruttori in Supersport, grazie alle prestazioni del nuovo Campione del Mondo Adrián Huertas (Aruba.it Racing WSSP Team) e al terzo posto di Yari Montella (Barni Spark Racing Team).

Un grazie di cuore a tutti i ragazzi e le ragazze di Ducati Corse: il loro impegno e la loro dedizione ci hanno permesso di festeggiare questi traguardi straordinari. Un ringraziamento speciale va anche a chi ha creduto in noi: i nostri sponsor e tutti coloro che hanno condiviso le nostre ambizioni.

Infine, grazie a tutti i Ducatisti, che con noi hanno sofferto e gioito.
#ForzaDucati

For the third consecutive year, the MotoGP World Champion is a Ducati rider!

After the World Championships won by Francesco Bagnaia in 2022 and 2023, this year it was Jorge Martín who wrote an important page in the history of motorcycle racing, on the Desmosedici GP of the Pramac Racing team. In 2024, which saw Ducati once again impose itself with record numbers, Jorge and Pecco gave extraordinary emotions to the fans. These two exceptional riders gave their all to compete for the title until the last race, continually raising the level of competition to prove who was the best. They showcased not only their extraordinary talent, but also a style, a philosophy, a working method, a team spirit and a way of winning that represent the beating heart of Ducati Corse.

In the end, it was Martín who won the world title, fulfilling his dream of becoming Champion, holding his own against an amazing Bagnaia who scored 11 wins this season. In addition to Bagnaia and Martín, Marc Márquez (Gresini Racing MotoGP) and Enea Bastianini thrilled all the Ducatisti, fighting until the end for the third step of the world championship podium.

A round of applause, then, to our Fantastic 4, the architects of the 19 victories obtained by Ducati this season. An absolute record not only for us, but also for MotoGP, with a Desmosedici GP that climbed to the top step of the podium in all the races of the 2024 calendar, except one. This year we achieved historic and significant milestones, such as the 100th victory in the premier class, which came in our home race in Misano, in the heart of the Motor Valley, thanks to Enea Bastianini in the Emilia-Romagna GP. Just one week later, in Indonesia, we celebrated our 100th pole position in MotoGP, with a total of 16 poles obtained by Ducati this year.

2024 was truly a memorable year: our best season ever in the premier class, embellished by the victory of our sixth Constructors' title (the fifth in a row) and the Teams' world title with the official Ducati Lenovo Team.
Once again, we confirmed the strength of our project, also thanks to the commitment and team spirit of our eight riders and four satellite teams: Francesco Bagnaia and Enea Bastianini; Jorge Martín and Franco Morbidelli (Pramac Racing); Marc and Alex Márquez (Gresini Racing MotoGP); Marco Bezzecchi and Fabio Di Giannantonio (VR46 Racing Team). A special thank you to all of them for allowing us to grow and reach these extraordinary goals.

The MotoGP World Championship crowns an exceptional racing season, in which we also won the Manufacturers' and Teams' titles in Superbike with the official riders of the Aruba.it – Racing Ducati Team, Nicolò Bulega and Álvaro Bautista, respectively second and third overall. We also won the Riders' and Manufacturers' titles in Supersport, thanks to the performances of the new World Champion Adrián Huertas (Aruba.it Racing WSSP Team) and the third place of Yari Montella (Barni Spark Racing Team).

A heartfelt thank you to all the men and women of Ducati Corse: their commitment and dedication have allowed us to celebrate these extraordinary goals. A special thank you also goes to those who believed in us: our sponsors and all those who shared our ambitions.

Finally, thanks to all the Ducatisti, who suffered and rejoiced with us.
#ForzaDucati

Luigi Dall'Igna
Ducati Corse General Manager

DUCATI
CORSE
Madonna di Campiglio
Trentino
MADONNA
DI CAMPIGLIO
Audi
Lenovo
aruba.it

TRENTINO
CAMPIONI
IN PISTA
Madonna di Campiglio
Trentino
Lenovo
aruba.it
Audi Sport
MONSTER

CAMPIONI
IN PISTA
Madonna di Campiglio
Trentino
DUCATI

TRENTINO
Audi

Lenovo
GIVI
23

DUCATI CORSE

77
222

Ducati Lenovo Team Presentation

22 January 2024
Madonna di Campiglio,
Trentino | Italy

2024 FIM MotoGP World Championship Calendar

1 Grand Prix of Qatar
2 Grande Prémio de Portugal
3 Grand Prix of The Americas
4 Gran Premio de España
5 Grand Prix de France
6 Gran Premi de Catalunya
7 Gran Premio d'Italia
8 TT Assen
9 Motorrad Grand Prix Deutschland
10 British Grand Prix
11 Motorrad Grand Prix von Österreich
12 Gran Premio de Aragón
13 Gran Premio di San Marino
e della Riviera di Rimini
14 Gran Premio dell'Emilia-Romagna
15 Grand Prix of Indonesia
16 Grand Prix of Japan
17 Australian Motorcycle Grand Prix
18 Grand Prix of Thailand
19 Grand Prix of Malaysia
20 Grand Prix of Barcelona

1|20

8-10 March | Qatar

Grand Prix of Qatar

Lusail International Circuit

Sprint Race	1. **Martín (Ducati)** 2. Binder (KTM) 3. A. Espargaró (Aprilia)
Race	1. **Bagnaia (Ducati)** 2. Binder (KTM) 3. **Martín (Ducati)**

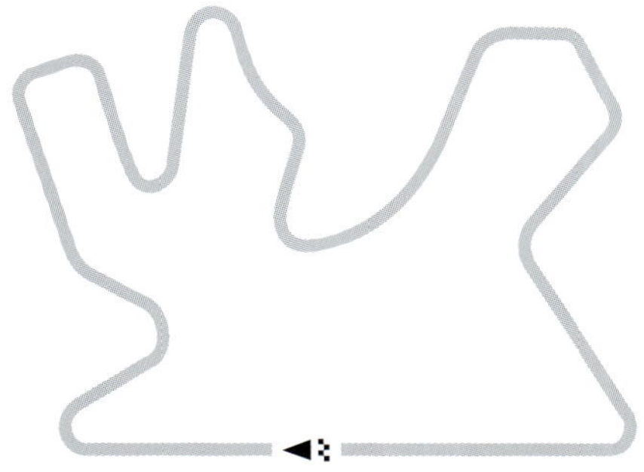

All Time Lap Record	Martín (Ducati) 1m50.789s (174.8 km/h) – 2024
Best Race Lap	Acosta (KTM) 1m52.657s (171.9 km/h) – 2024
Top Speed	Zarco (Ducati) 362.4 km/h – 2021
Track Length	5.380 km
Corners	16 (6 left, 10 right)
Race Distance	1 x 11 laps (59.18 km), 1 x 21 laps (112.98 km)

Step on board

21
QATAR AIRWAY
QATAR AIRWAYS

prima
PRAMAC
Lenovo

riello
Lenovo
DAIKO
63
1

riello
ADVANCE
Lenovo
FRECCIAROSSA
TIM
VARGROUP
CARRERA
MONSTER ENERGY
riello
FRECCIAROSSA
Lenovo
CARRERA
TIM
Lenovo
SUOMY
Lenovo
UnipolSai

22-24 March | Portugal

Grande Prémio de Portugal

Autódromo Internacional do Algarve

Sprint Race	1. Viñales (Aprilia) 2. M. Márquez (Ducati) 3. Martín (Ducati)
Race	1. Martín (Ducati) 2. Bastianini (Ducati) 3. Acosta (KTM)

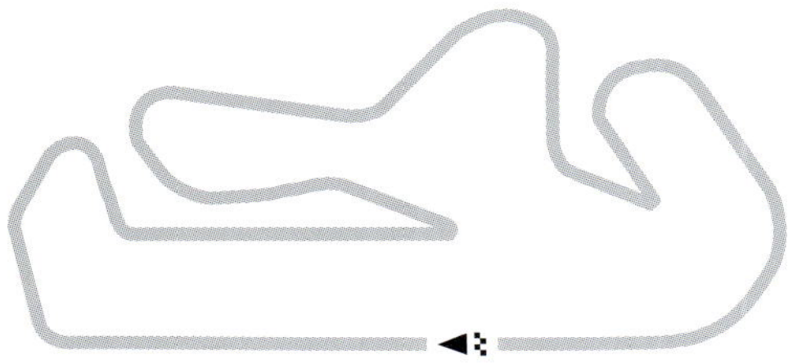

All Time Lap Record	M. Márquez (Honda) 1m37.226s (170.0 km/h) – 2023
Best Race Lap	Bastianini (Ducati) 1m38.685s (167.5 km/h) – 2024
Top Speed	Oliveira (Aprilia) 352.9 km/h – 2024
Track Length	4.592 km
Corners	15 (6 left, 9 right)
Race Distance	1 x 12 laps (55.104 km), 1 x 25 laps (114.8 km)

Step on board

Lenovo

Lenovo
NetApp
MONSTER ENERGY
FRECCIAROSSA

3|20

12-14 April | USA

Grand Prix of The Americas

Circuit Of The Americas

Sprint Race	1. Viñales (Aprilia) 2. M. Márquez (Ducati) 3. Martín (Ducati)
Race	1. Viñales (Aprilia) 2. Acosta (KTM) 3. Bastianini (Ducati)

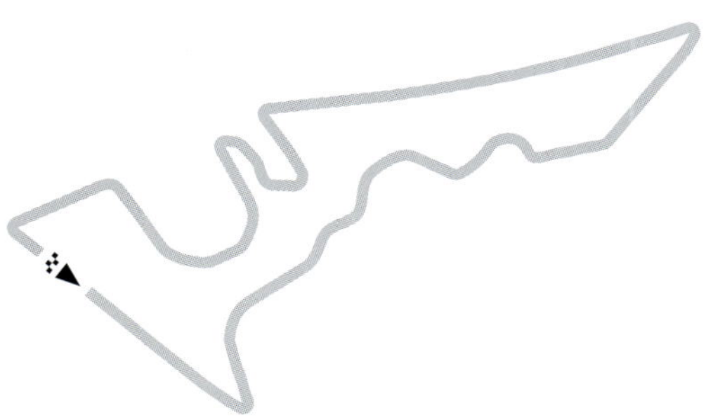

All Time Lap Record	Viñales (Aprilia) 2m00.864s (164.2 km/h) – 2024
Best Race Lap	Viñales (Aprilia) 2m02.575s (161.9 km/h) – 2024
Top Speed	Viñales (Aprilia) 356.4 km/h – 2023
Track Length	5.513 km
Corners	20 (11 left, 9 right)
Race Distance	1 x 10 laps (55.13 km), 1 x 20 laps (110.26 km)

Step on board

#3

23
Lenovo

TIM
riello
FLEX-BOX
Lenovo
DUCATI
DUCATI CORSE
AKRAPOVIC
GIVI
Lenovo
SIEMENS
streparava
elica
MICHELIN
Reflexallen
D.I.D

TISSOT
TISSOT
TISSOT
Antangin
DAIKO
DUCATI

63
Lenovo
alpinestars
Lenovo

4 | 20

26-28 April | Spain

Gran Premio de España

Circuito de Jerez – Ángel Nieto

Sprint Race	1. Martín (Ducati) 2. Acosta (KTM) 3. Pedrosa (KTM)
Race	1. Bagnaia (Ducati) 2. M. Márquez (Ducati) 3. Bezzecchi (Ducati)

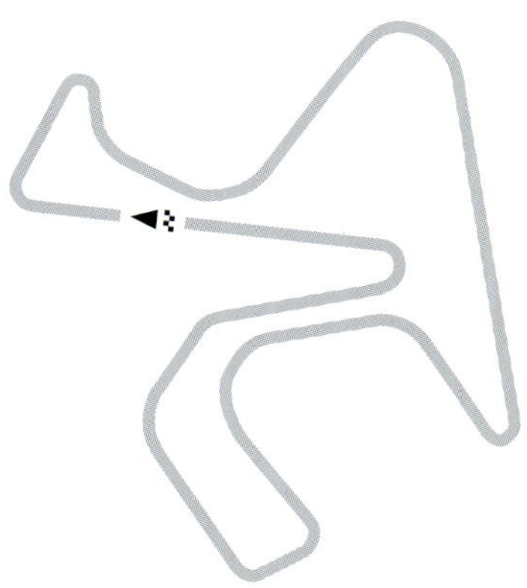

All Time Lap Record	Bagnaia (Ducati) 1m36.025s (165.8 km/h) – 2024
Best Race Lap	Bagnaia (Ducati) 1m37.449s (163.3 km/h) – 2024
Top Speed	Zarco (Ducati) 300.8 km/h – 2021
Track Length	4.423 km
Corners	13 (5 left, 8 right)
Race Distance	1 x 12 laps (53.076 km), 1 x 25 laps (110.575 km)

Step on board

REMIO
MICHELIN
Lenovo
motorola
Lenovo
Lenovo

GRAN PREMIO ESTRELLA GALICIA 0,0 DE ESPAÑA 2024
72 Marco BEZZECCHI
49 Fabio DI GIANNANTONIO
DUCATI CORSE

ÖHLINS
FACTORY RACING
Enduro

TIM
Lenovo
GIVI
MICHELIN

Lenovo
Audi Sport
MICHELIN

10-12 May | France

Grand Prix de France

Le Mans

Sprint Race	1. Martín (Ducati) 2. M. Márquez (Ducati) 3. Viñales (Aprilia)
Race	1. Martín (Ducati) 2. M. Márquez (Ducati) 3. Bagnaia (Ducati)

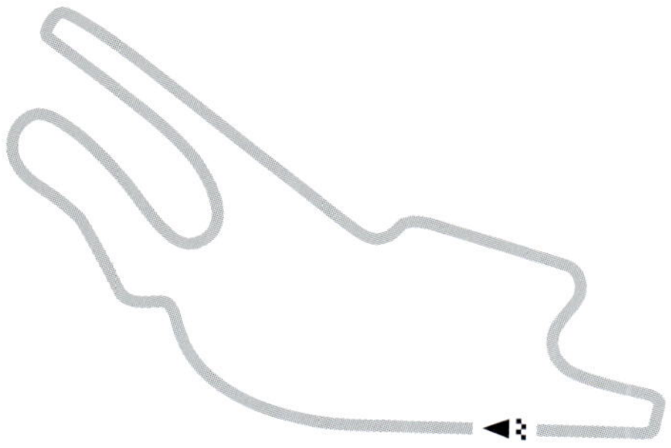

All Time Lap Record	Martín (Ducati) 1m29.919s (167.5 km/h) – 2024
Best Race Lap	Bastianini (Ducati) 1m31.107s (165.3 km/h) – 2024
Top Speed	Binder (KTM) 325.8 km/h – 2023
Track Length	4.19 km
Corners	14 (5 left, 9 right)
Race Distance	1 x 13 laps (54.405 km), 1 x 27 laps (112.995 km)

Step on board

MICHELIN
MICHELIN
MICHELIN
MICHELIN® GRAND PRIX DE FRANCE 2024

PIT LANE

MICHELIN
MICHELIN
MICHELIN
Lenovo
89
prima

24-26 May | Spain

Gran Premi de Catalunya

Circuit de Barcelona-Catalunya

Sprint Race	1. A. Espargaró (Aprilia) 2. M. Márquez (Ducati) 3. Acosta (KTM)
Race	1. Bagnaia (Ducati) 2. Martín (Ducati) 3. M. Márquez (Ducati)

All Time Lap Record	A. Espargaró (Aprilia) 1m38.190s (170.7 km/h) – 2024
Best Race Lap	Acosta (KTM) 1m39.664s (168.2 km/h) – 2024
Top Speed	Morbidelli (Ducati) 356.4 km/h – 2024
Track Length	4.657 km
Corners	14 (6 left, 8 right)
Race Distance	1 x 12 laps (55.884 km), 1 x 24 laps (111.768 km)

Step on board

Lenovo
NetApp
MONSTER ENERGY
FRECCIAROSSA
DAIKO
MICHELIN
alpinestars
Lenovo
motorola
Unibal
ASPIRA
RACING
Antangin

Lenovo
UnipolSai

MONSTER
ENERGY

Lenovo
riello
FRECCIAROSSA
CARRERA
VARGROUP
TIM
Lenovo
riello
FRECCIAROSSA
CARRERA

31 May - 2 June | Italy

Gran Premio d'Italia

Autodromo Internazionale del Mugello

Sprint Race	1. Bagnaia (Ducati) 2. M. Márquez (Ducati) 3. Acosta (KTM)
Race	1. Bagnaia (Ducati) 2. Bastianini (Ducati) 3. Martín (Ducati)

All Time Lap Record	Martín (Ducati) 1m44.504s (180.6 km/h) – 2024
Best Race Lap	Bagnaia (Ducati) 1m45.770s (178.5 km/h) – 2024
Top Speed	Binder (KTM) 366.1 km/h – 2023
Track Length	5.245 km
Corners	15 (6 left, 9 right)
Race Distance	1 x 11 laps (57.695 km), 1 x 23 laps (120.635 km)

Step on board

Lenovo
BARANA
HERNANDEZ
DALL'IGNA
GRASSILLI
POGGIA
TOMASSINI
VENTURA
POGGI
DAVOLI
BARALDINI
OLIVI
DE CASSAN
BRAIATO
COSTANTINI
ROMELE
CASOLARI
INTURRISI
NABALINI
VILALTA
TARDOZZI
BAGNAIA
SIMONCINI
SACCONELLI
MASSARIN

Lenovo
NetApp
MONSTER
FRECCIAROSSA
DAIKO
Lenovo
UnipolSai
DAIKO
MICHELIN
2

Lenovo
riello

Lenovo
UnipolSai
NetApp
DAIKO

Lenovo
NetApp
elica

8 | 20

28-30 June | Netherlands

TT Assen

TT Circuit Assen

Sprint Race	1. Bagnaia (Ducati) 2. Martín (Ducati) 3. Viñales (Aprilia)
Race	1. Bagnaia (Ducati) 2. Martín (Ducati) 3. Bastianini (Ducati)

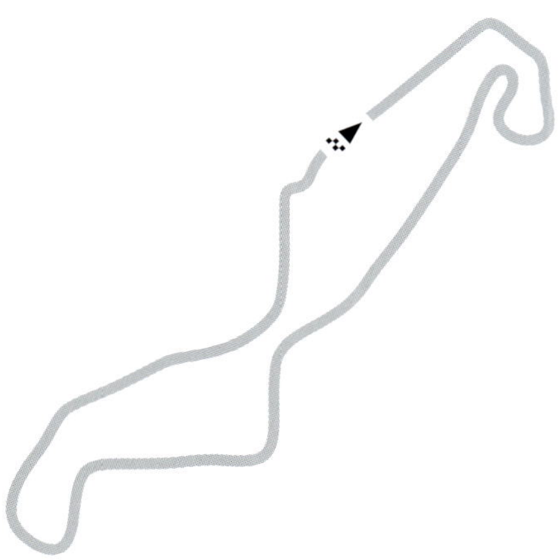

All Time Lap Record	Bagnaia (Ducati) 1m30.540s (180.5 km/h) – 2024
Best Race Lap	Bagnaia (Ducati) 1m31.866s (177.9 km/h) – 2024
Top Speed	Iannone (Ducati) 319.8 km/h – 2015
Track Length	4.542 km
Corners	18 (6 left, 12 right)
Race Distance	1 x 13 laps (59.046 km), 1 x 26 laps (118.092 km)

Step on board

MICHELIN
Lenovo
NetApp
UnipolSai
FRECCIAROSSA

Lenovo
riello
TIM
CARRERA
VARGROUP
FRECCIAROSSA
Lenovo
SUOMY

5-7 July | Germany

Motorrad Grand Prix Deutschland

Sachsenring

Sprint Race	1. Martín (Ducati) 2. Oliveira (Aprilia) 3. Bagnaia (Ducati)
Race	1. Bagnaia (Ducati) 2. M. Márquez (Ducati) 3. A. Márquez (Ducati)

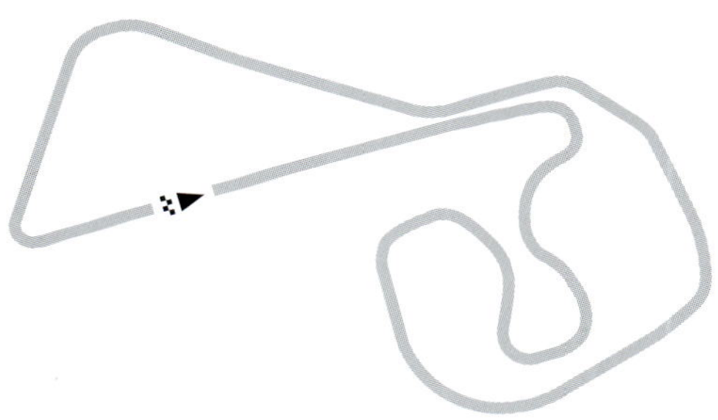

All Time Lap Record	Martín (Ducati) 1m19.423s (166.3 km/h) – 2024
Best Race Lap	Martín (Ducati) 1m20.667s (163.8 km/h) – 2024
Top Speed	Acosta (KTM) 306.8 km/h – 2024
Track Length	3.671 km
Corners	13 (10 left, 3 right)
Race Distance	1 x 15 laps (55.065 km), 1 x 30 laps (110.13 km)

Step on board

LIQUI MOLY
LIQUI MOLY
LIQUI MOLY
LIQUI MOLY
LIQUI MOLY
TIM
riello ups
Lenovo
Lenovo
Lenovo
Lenovo
riello
ADVANCE
MICHELIN
Audi Sport

LIQUI MOLY
LIQUI MOLY MOTO
GRAND PRIX DEUTS
Sachsenring

200
GP

10 | 20

2-4 August | Britain

British Grand Prix

Silverstone Circuit

Sprint Race	1. Bastianini (Ducati) 2. Martín (Ducati) 3. A.Espargaró (Aprilia)
Race	1. Bastianini (Ducati) 2. Martín (Ducati) 3. Bagnaia (Ducati)

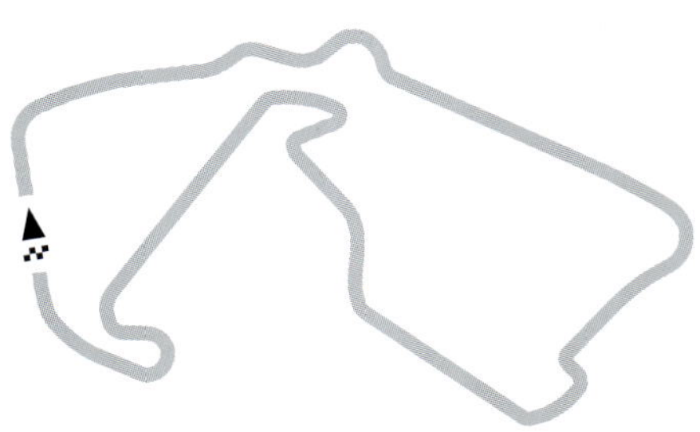

All Time Lap Record	A. Espargaró (Aprilia) 1m57.309s (181.0 km/h) – 2024
Best Race Lap	A. Espargaró (Aprilia) 1m58.895s (178.6 km/h) – 2024
Top Speed	Bastianini (Ducati) 340.6 km/h – 2022
Track Length	5.9 km
Corners	18 (8 left, 10 right)
Race Distance	1 x 10 laps (59.00 km), 1 x 20 laps (118.00 km)

Step on board

MICHELIN
KYT
Lenovo
alpinestars
TIM
Lenovo
motorola
riello
CARRERA
SAP
Lenovo
KYT
Lenovo
NetApp

HISTORY NEVER ENDS
MONSTER ENERGY BRITISH GRAND PRIX 2024
PROSECCO DOC

LIQUI
MOLY
Lenovo
23

Lenovo
alpinestars
MICHELIN

11|20

16-18 August | Austria

Motorrad Grand Prix von Österreich

Red Bull Ring - Spielberg

Sprint Race	1. Bagnaia (Ducati) 2. Martín (Ducati) 3. A.Espargaró (Aprilia)
Race	1. Bagnaia (Ducati) 2. Martín (Ducati) 3. Bastianini (Ducati)

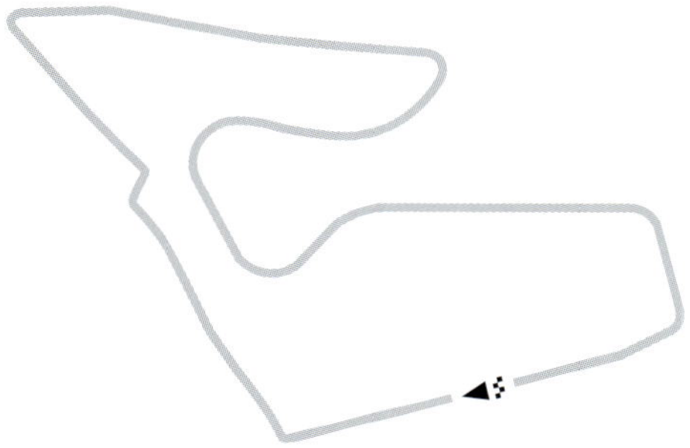

All Time Lap Record	Martín (Ducati) 1m27.748s (178.3 km/h) – 2024
Best Race Lap	Bagnaia (Ducati) 1m29.840 (174.2 km/h) – 2023
Top Speed	Savadori (Aprilia) 317.1 km/h – 2024
Track Length	4.35 km
Corners	11 (3 left, 8 right)
Race Distance	1 x 14 laps (60.872 km), 1 x 28 laps (121.744 km)

Step on board

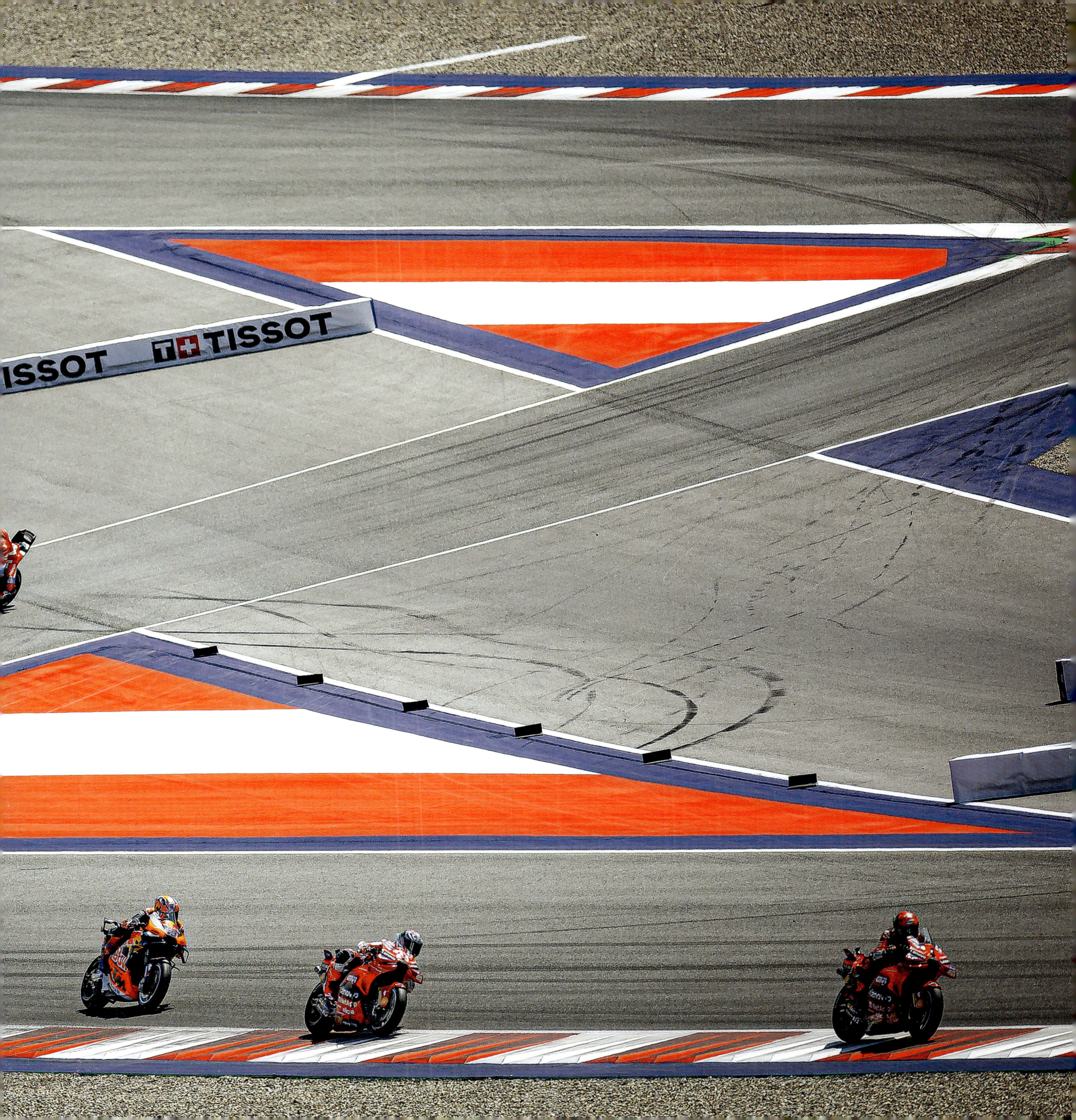
ISSOT
TISSOT

TISSOT
SINGHA

TIM
riello
Lenovo
ADVANCE
DAIKO

RACING FOR THE FUTURE
RACING FOR THE FUTURE
UnipolSai
lenovo
elica
riello
MICHELIN
motoGP

12 | 20

30 August - 1 September | Spain

Gran Premio de Aragón

MotorLand Aragón

Sprint Race
1. **M. Márquez (Ducati)**
2. **Martín (Ducati)**
3. Acosta (KTM)

Race
1. **M. Márquez (Ducati)**
2. **Martín (Ducati)**
3. Acosta (KTM)

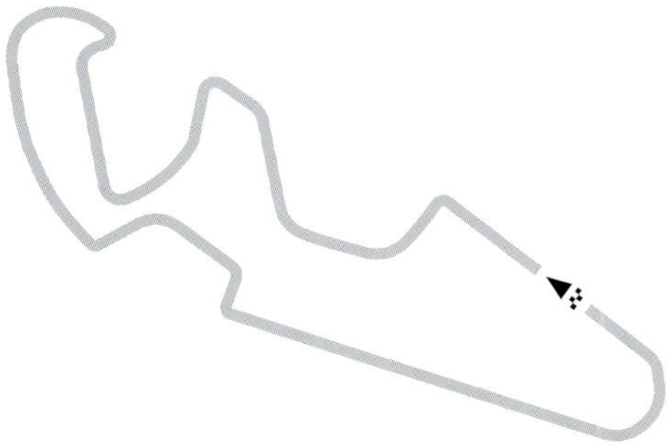

All Time Lap Record	M. Márquez (Ducati) 1m45.801s (172.7 km/h) – 2024
Best Race Lap	Marini (Ducati) 1m47.795 (169.5 km/h) – 2022
Top Speed	Bastianini (Ducati) 354.1 km/h – 2022
Track Length	5.08 km
Corners	17 (10 left, 7 right)
Race Distance	1 x 11 laps (55.847 km), 1 x 23 laps (116.771 km)

Step on board

SHOEI
Antangin
YOU-ALL
Estrella Galicia
Unibat
Kapriol
93
Gigetta
FEDERAL OIL
Wonderful Indonesia

Lenovo
DUCATI
riello
aruba.it
FRECCIAROSSA
VARGROUP
TIM
NetApp
UnipolSai
CARRERA
MICHELIN
AKRAPOVIC

Lenovo

63
riello

6-8 September | Italy

Gran Premio di San Marino e della Riviera di Rimini

Misano World Circuit
Marco Simoncelli

Sprint Race

1. Martín (Ducati)
2. Bagnaia (Ducati)
3. Morbidelli (Ducati)

Race

1. M. Márquez (Ducati)
2. Bagnaia (Ducati)
3. Bastianini (Ducati)

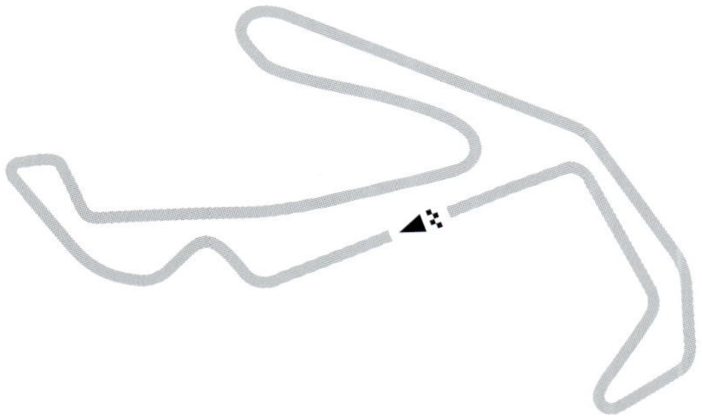

All Time Lap Record	Bagnaia (Ducati) 1m30.304s (168.4 km/h) – 2024
Best Race Lap	M. Márquez (Ducati) 1m31.564s (166.1 km/h) – 2024
Top Speed	Bezzecchi (Ducati) 305.9 km/h – 2023
Track Length	4.226 km
Corners	16 (6 left, 10 right)
Race Distance	1 x 13 laps (54.938 km), 1 x 27 laps (114.102 km)

Step on board

Bull

Lenovo
riello
TIM
ADVANCE
FRECCIAROSSA
SUOMY
Audi Sport
MICHELIN

MICHELIN
MICHELIN
MICHELIN
DUCATI
93
riello
elica
MICHELIN

14 | 20

20-22 September | Italy

Gran Premio dell'Emilia-Romagna

Misano World Circuit
Marco Simoncelli

Sprint Race	1. Bagnaia (Ducati) 2. Martín (Ducati) 3. Bastianini (Ducati)
Race	1. Bastianini (Ducati) 2. Martín (Ducati) 3. M. Márquez (Ducati)

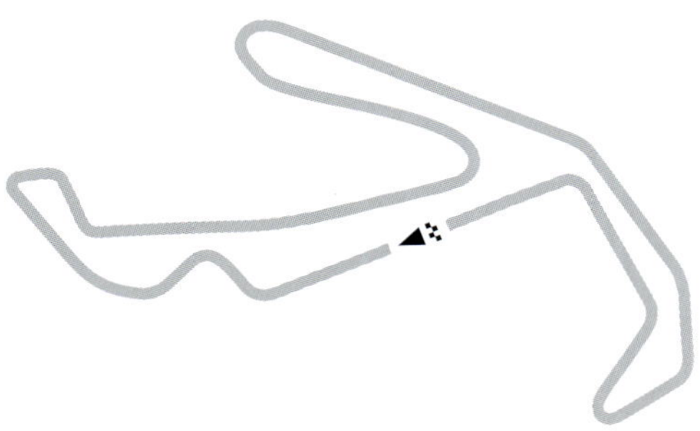

All Time Lap Record	Bagnaia (Ducati) 1m30.031s (168.9 km/h) – 2024
Best Race Lap	Bagnaia (Ducati) 1m30.877s (167.4 km/h) – 2024
Top Speed	Bezzecchi (Ducati) 305.9 km/h – 2023
Track Length	4.226 km
Corners	16 (6 left, 10 right)
Race Distance	1 x 13 laps (54.938 km), 1 x 27 laps (114.102 km)

Step on board

TERRANOVA
23
Lenovo
riello
TIM
FRECCIAROSSA
VARGROUP
MONSTER ENERGY
CARRERA
aruba.it

PRAMA
PRAMAC
PRAMAC

GRAN PREMIO PRAMAC
DUCATI
CORSE
100 GP WINS
2003 | 2024
DUCATI
CORSE
MotoGP™
2024
CONSTRUCTORS'
WORLD CHAMPION

15 | 20

27-29 September | Indonesia

Grand Prix of Indonesia

Mandalika International Circuit

Sprint Race	1. Bagnaia (Ducati) 2. Bastianini (Ducati) 3. M. Márquez (Ducati)
Race	1. Martín (Ducati) 2. Acosta (KTM) 3. Bagnaia (Ducati)

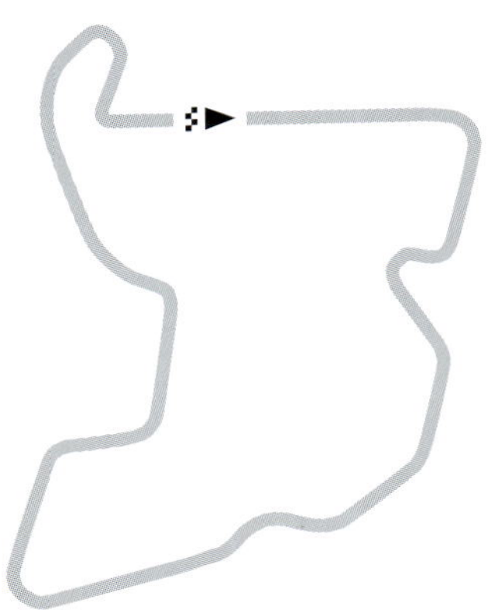

All Time Lap Record	Martín (Ducati) 1m29.088s (173.8 km/h) – 2024
Best Race Lap	Bastianini (Ducati) 1m30.539s (171.0 km/h) – 2024
Top Speed	Acosta (KTM) 319.5 km/h – 2024
Track Length	4.3 km
Corners	17 (6 left, 11 right)
Race Distance	1 x 13 laps (55.913 km), 1 x 27 laps (116.13 km)

Step on board

SUOMY
Lenovo
CARRERA
riello
ADVANCE
VARGROUP
FRECCIAROSSA
PECCO
MONSTER ENERGY
TIM
Sport
DAIKO
GIVI
UnipolSai
NetApp
elica
alpinestars

SUOMY
Lenovo
NetApp
MONSTER ENERGY
UnipolSai
riello
CARRERA
TIM
alpinestars

23
riello
Lenovo
93
Estrella Galicia 0,0
Unibat
SHOEI

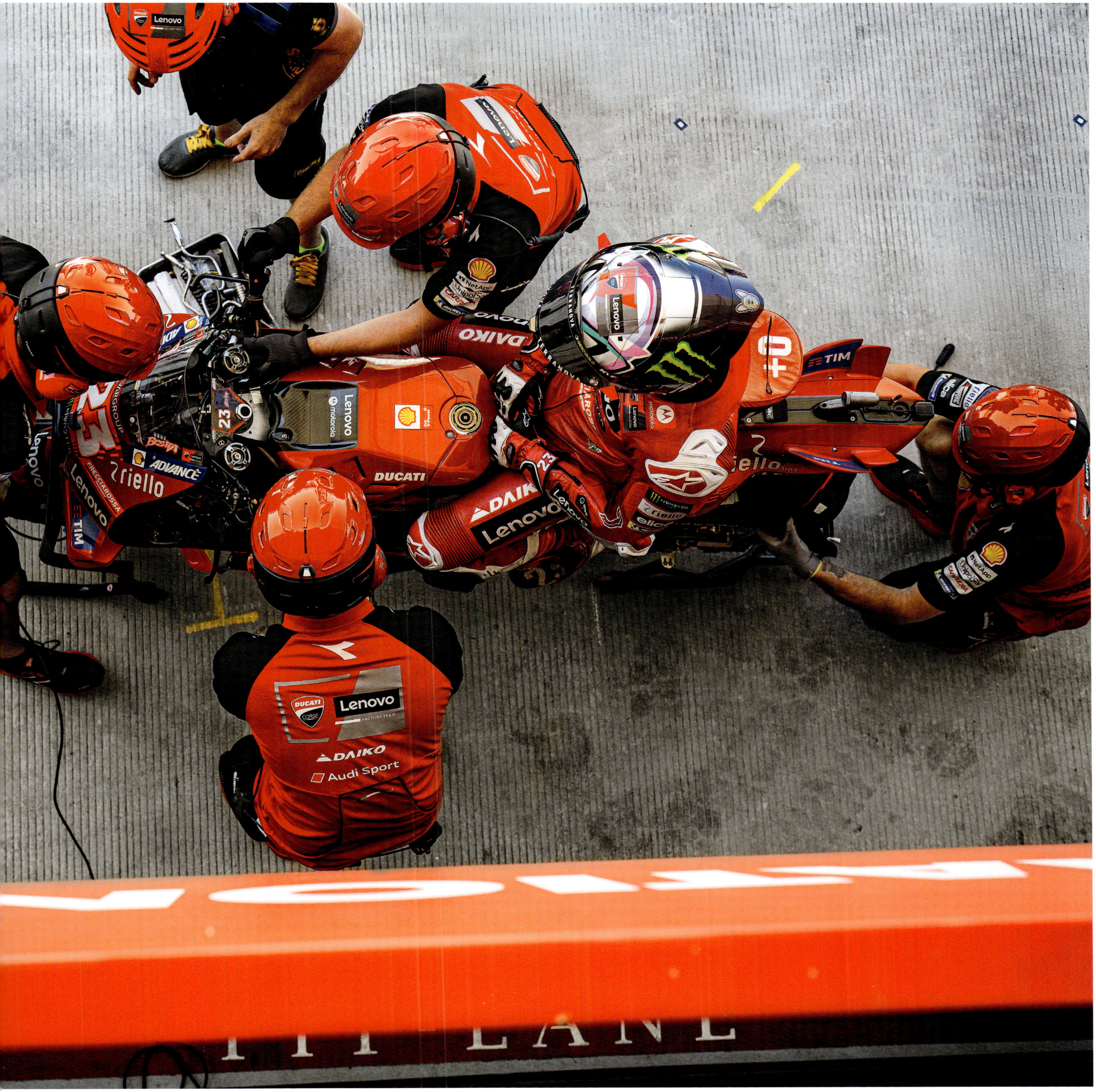

4-6 October | Japan

Grand Prix of Japan

Mobility Resort Motegi

Sprint Race	1. Bagnaia (Ducati) 2. Bastianini (Ducati) 3. M. Márquez (Ducati)
Race	1. Bagnaia (Ducati) 2. Martín (Ducati) 3. M. Márquez (Ducati)

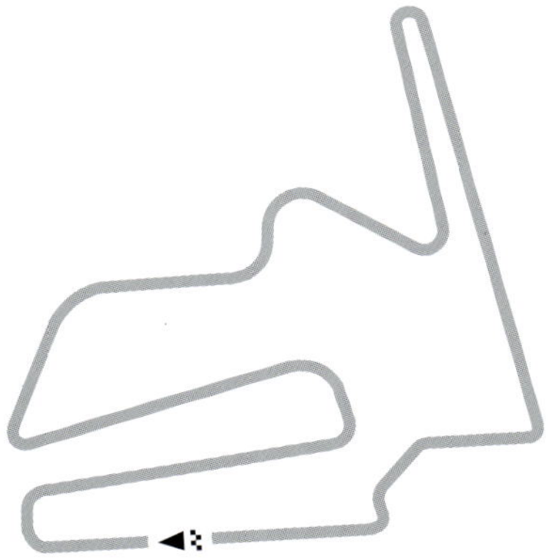

All Time Lap Record	Acosta (KTM) 1m43.018s (167.7 km/h) – 2024
Best Race Lap	Martín (Ducati) 1m44.461s (165.4 km/h) – 2024
Top Speed	Bastianini (Ducati) 317.6 km/h – 2022
Track Length	4.8 km
Corners	14 (6 left, 8 right)
Race Distance	1 x 12 laps (57.612 km), 1 x 24 laps (115.224 km)

Step on board

Lenovo
33
KTM
31
GASGAS
23
Lenovo
49
20

Lenovo
Join us on

Lenovo
TIM
riello
AKRAPOVIC
elica
MICHELIN

SUOMY
Lenovo
riello
CARRERA
FRECCIAROSSA

KYT
VARGROUP
riello
23
FRECCIAROSSA
Lenovo
TIM
aruba.it

Lenovo
VARGROUP
23
riello
FRECCIAROSSA
Lenovo
TIM

17|20

18-20 October | Australia

Australian Motorcycle Grand Prix

Phillip Island Grand Prix Circuit

Sprint Race	1. Martín (Ducati) 2. M. Márquez (Ducati) 3. Bastianini (Ducati)
Race	1. M. Márquez (Ducati) 2. Martín (Ducati) 3. Bagnaia (Ducati)

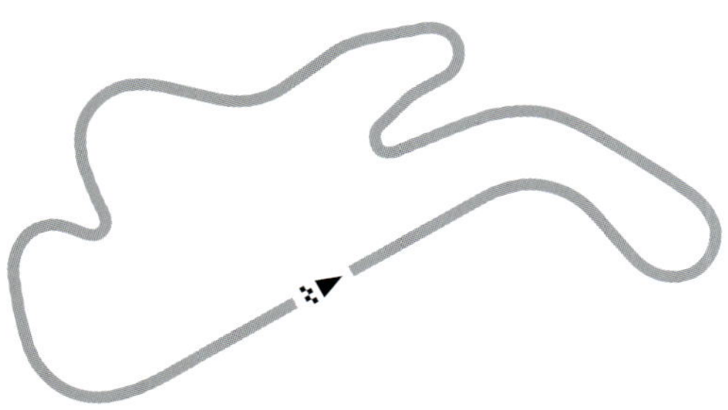

All Time Lap Record	Martín (Ducati) 1m27.246s (183.5 km/h) – 2023
Best Race Lap	M. Márquez (Ducati) 1m27.765s (182.4 km/h) – 2024
Top Speed	Bastianini (Ducati) 356.4 km/h – 2022
Track Length	4.45 km
Corners	12 (7 left, 5 right)
Race Distance	1 x 13 laps (57.824 km), 1 x 27 laps (120.096 km)

Step on board

PHILLIP ISLAND CIRCUIT
MELBOURNE
MELBOURNE
IRWAYS
QATAR AIRWAYS

riello
elica
MICHELIN
Lenovo

Lenovo

QATAR
AIRWAYS
QATAR AIRWAYS AUSTRALIAN
MOTORCYCLE GRAND PRIX 20
Phillip Island

18 | 20

25-27 October | Thailand

Grand Prix of Thailand

Chang International Circuit

Sprint Race	1. Bastianini (Ducati) 2. Martín (Ducati) 3. Bagnaia (Ducati)
Race	1. Bagnaia (Ducati) 2. Martín (Ducati) 3. Acosta (KTM)

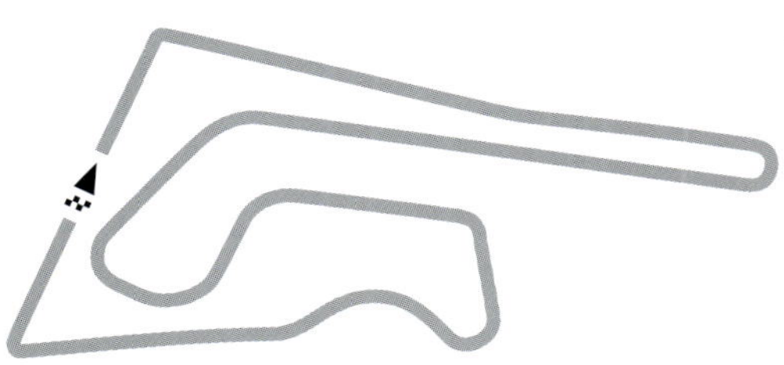

All Time Lap Record	Bagnaia (Ducati) 1m28.700s (184.8 km/h) – 2024
Best Race Lap	Bezzecchi (Ducati) 1m30.896s (180.3 km/h) – 2023
Top Speed	Martín (Ducati) 338.5 km/h – 2024
Track Length	4.55 km
Corners	12 (5 left, 7 right)
Race Distance	1 x 13 laps (59.202 km), 1 x 26 laps (118.404 km)

Step on board

INTERNATION
PRAMAC
riello
ebay
Enduro
DUCATI

DUCATI CORSE
Lenovo
FACTORY TEAM
MotoGP™
2024
TEAM
WORLD CHAMPION

23
Lenovo
riello

PT GRA
OF THA
Chang International
MICHELIN
Lenovo
NetApp
MONSTER
FRECCIAROSSA

enovo
riello
Audi Sport
MICHELIN

19 | 20

1-3 November | Malaysia

Grand Prix of Malaysia

Sepang International Circuit

Sprint Race	1. Martín (Ducati) 2. M. Márquez (Ducati) 3. Bastianini (Ducati)
Race	1. Bagnaia (Ducati) 2. Martín (Ducati) 3. Bastianini (Ducati)

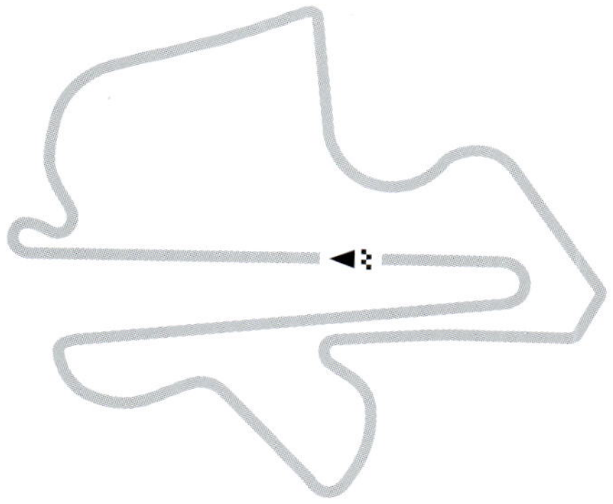

All Time Lap Record	Bagnaia (Ducati) 1m56.337s (171.5 km/h) – 2024
Best Race Lap	A. Márquez (Ducati) 1m58.979s (167.7 km/h) – 2023
Top Speed	Iannone (Ducati) 339.6 km/h – 2015
Track Length	5.54 km
Corners	15 (5 left, 10 right)
Race Distance	1 x 10 laps (55.43 km), 1 x 19 laps (105.317 km)

Step on board

PETRONAS
50 YEARS

Lenovo
NetApp
FIM MotoGP
WORLD CHAMPIONSHIP
TOWER OF CHAMPIONS
75
prima
PRAMAC

PETRONAS
50

riello
Lenovo
TIM
FRECCIAROSSA
VARGROUP
ADVANCE
MONSTER
SUOMY
PRAMAC
prima
LINO SONEGO
MOTUL
Red Bull

20|20

15-17 November | Spain

Grand Prix of Barcelona

Circuit de Barcelona-Catalunya

Sprint Race	1. Bagnaia (Ducati) 2. Bastianini (Ducati) 3. Martín (Ducati)
Race	1. Bagnaia (Ducati) 2. M. Márquez (Ducati) 3. Martín (Ducati)

All Time Lap Record	A. Espargarò (Aprilia) 1m38.190s (170.7 km/h) – 2024
Best Race Lap	Acosta (KTM) 1m39.664s (168.2 km/h) – 2024
Top Speed	Morbidelli (Ducati) 356.4 km/h – 2024
Track Length	4.66 km
Corners	14 (6 left, 8 right)
Race Distance	1 x 12 laps (55.884 km), 1 x 24 laps (111.768 km)

Step on board

JORGE
MARTIN
89
2024
WORLD
CHAMPION
PRAMAC
DUCATI

prima
PRAMAC
MOTUL
89
Lenovo
NetApp
elica
GIVI

93
89

89
Lenovo

prima
PRAMAC
Audi Sport
MICHELIN
alpinestars
WORLD CHAMPION 2024

Title Partner

Main Partners

Official Sponsors

Grazie a chi ha corso con noi tutto l'anno / Thanks to those who raced with us all year

Official Partners

aruba.it · Autogrill · Bosch · Carrera · Contadi Castaldi · Daiko · Diadora · Eataly · Flex-Box · Frecciarossa · Givi · MAN · Melinda · Montenegro · Motorola · Parmacotto · Philip Morris International · Randstad

Technical Partners

Beta · Brembo · Cobo · D.I.D · Domino · Mahle · Marelli · NGK · Reflexallen · Siemens · Streparava · Thermal Technology · Var Group · WD-40 · SAP · Vmoto

Ducati Desmosedici GP 2024

Motore / Engine	4 tempi, V4 a 90°, raffreddato a liquido, distribuzione desmodromica con doppio albero a camme in testa, 4 valvole per cilindro / Liquid-cooled, 90° V4, four-stroke, Desmodromic DOHC, four valves per cylinder
Cilindrata / Capacity	1.000 cc / 1,000 cc
Potenza massima / Maximum power	Oltre 250 cv / Over 250 hp
Velocità massima / Maximum speed	Oltre 350km/h / Over 350 km/h (218 mph)
Trasmissione / Transmission	Ducati Seamless Transmission. Trasmissione finale a catena / Chain final drive
Alimentazione / Carburation	Iniezione elettronica indiretta, 4 corpi farfallati con iniettori sopra e sotto farfalla. Farfalle controllate da doppio sistema Ride By Wire / Indirect electronic injection, four throttle bodies with injectors above and below the butterfly valves. Throttles operated by double Ride by Wire systems
Carburante / Fuel	Shell Racing V-Power
Lubrificante / Lubricant	Shell Advance Ultra 4
Scarico / Exhaust	Akrapovič
Trasmissione finale / Final Drive	Catena D.I.D. / D.I.D. Chain
Telaio / Frame	Doppio trave in lega di alluminio / Aluminium alloy twin-spar
Sospensioni / Suspension	Forcella rovesciata Öhlins con foderi in carbonio e ammortizzatore posteriore Öhlins, con regolazione di precarico e freno idraulico in compressione ed estensione / Inverted front fork with carbon outer tubes and rear shock absorber, adjustable for preload and damping
Elettronica / Electronics	Centralina Marelli programmata con Software Unico Dorna / ECU programmed with Dorna Unified Software.
Pneumatici / Tyres	Michelin, su cerchi anteriore e posteriore Ø17" / 17" front and rear
Cerchioni / Wheel Rims	Marchesini in lega di magnesio / magnesium alloy
Impianto frenante / Brakes	Brembo, doppio disco anteriore in carbonio con pinze a quattro pistoncini. Disco posteriore singolo in acciaio con pinza a due pistoncini / Two carbon front discs with four-piston calipers. Single stainless steel rear disc with two-piston caliper
Peso a secco / Dry weight	157 kg (346.1 lbs.)

TIM
riello ups
FLEX-BOX
Lenovo
DUCATI
DUCATI CORSE
PECCO
riello
FRECCIAROSSA
Lenovo
TIM
CARRERA
DAIKO
Audi Spor
GIVI
Lenovo
NetA
SIEMENS
streparava
elica
MONSTER ENERGY
MARELLI
AKRAPOVIC
Reflexallen
D.I.D
MICHELIN

DUCATI CORSE

Lenovo FACTORY TEAM

Lenovo
NetApp
GIVI
elica
23

DUCATI
PRAMAC
DUCATI
Lenovo
FRECCIAROSSA

2024 MotoGP World Championship Classification

Position	Number	Rider	Nationality	Team	Points
1	89	Jorge Martín	SPA	Prima Pramac Racing	508
2	1	Francesco Bagnaia	ITA	Ducati Lenovo Team	498
3	93	Marc Márquez	SPA	Gresini Racing MotoGP	392
4	23	Enea Bastianini	ITA	Ducati Lenovo Team	386
5	33	Brad Binder	RSA	Red Bull KTM Factory Racing	217
6	31	Pedro Acosta	SPA	Red Bull GasGas Tech3	215
7	12	Maverick Viñales	SPA	Aprilia Racing	190
8	73	Alex Márquez	SPA	Gresini Racing MotoGP	173
9	21	Franco Morbidelli	ITA	Prima Pramac Racing	173
10	49	Fabio Di Giannantonio	ITA	Pertamina Enduro VR46 Racing Team	165
11	41	Aleix Espargaró	SPA	Aprilia Racing	163
12	72	Marco Bezzecchi	ITA	Pertamina Enduro VR46 Racing Team	153
13	20	Fabio Quartararo	FRA	Monster Energy Yamaha MotoGP Team	113
14	43	Jack Miller	AUS	Red Bull KTM Factory Racing	87
15	88	Miguel Oliveira	POR	Trackhouse Racing	75
16	25	Raúl Fernández	SPA	Trackhouse Racing	66
17	5	Johann Zarco	FRA	Castrol Honda LCR	55
18	42	Alex Rins	SPA	Monster Energy Yamaha MotoGP Team	31
19	30	Takaaki Nakagami	JPN	Idemitsu Honda LCR	31
20	37	Augusto Fernández	SPA	Red Bull GasGas Tech3	27

Constructors

Position	Constructor	Points
1	Ducati	722
2	KTM	327
3	Aprilia	302
4	Yamaha	124
5	Honda	75

Teams

Position	Team	Points
1	Ducati Lenovo Team	884
2	Prima Pramac Racing	681
3	Gresini Racing MotoGP	565
4	Aprilia Racing	353
5	Pertamina Enduro VR46 Racing Team	318
6	Red Bull KTM Factory Racing	304
7	Red Bull GasGas Tech3	242
8	Monster Energy Yamaha MotoGP	144
9	Trackhouse Racing	141
10	LCR Honda	86

Francesco Bagnaia

Ducati Lenovo Team

Age:	27 (Born 14th January 1997)
Birthplace:	Turin (Italy)
Bike:	Ducati Desmosedici GP
Race number:	1
GPs started:	106
First GP:	Qatar 2019
Wins:	29
First win:	Aragón 2021
Pole positions:	24
First pole:	Qatar 2021
Fastest laps:	19
Points:	1583
Titles:	MotoGP (2022, 2023), Moto2 (2018)

2024 Season

Final position:	2nd
Points:	498
Wins:	11

PECCO

Lenovo
TIM
CARRERA

SUOMY
Lenovo
TIM
CARRERA
Audi Sport

CARRERA
EYEWEAR SINCE 1956
Lenovo
TIM

1
63

TIM
riello
Lenovo
Audi Sport
ADVANCE

Enea Bastianini

Ducati Lenovo Team

Age:	26 (Born 30th December 1997)
Birthplace:	Rimini (Italy)
Bike:	Ducati Desmosedici GP
Race number:	23
GPs started:	69
First GP:	Qatar 2022
Wins:	7
First win:	Qatar 2022
Pole positions:	2
First pole:	Austria 2022
Fastest laps:	9
Points:	791
Titles:	Moto2 (2020), RS125 GP (2012)

2024 Season

Final position:	4th
Points:	386
Wins:	2

23
Lenovo
riello
FRECCIAROSSA
TIM
ADVANCE
VARGROUP

Lenovo
FACTORY TEAM

23
Lenovo
riello
VARGROUP
FRECCIAROSSA
TIM
CARRERA
MONSTER

23

Lenovo
GIVI
NetApp
elica
DAIKO
SIEMENS
riello

Jorge Martín

Prima Pramac Racing

Age:	26 (Born 29th January 1998)
Birthplace:	Madrid (Spain)
Bike:	Ducati Desmosedici GP
Race number:	89
GPs started:	74
First GP:	Qatar 2021
Wins:	8
First win:	Styria 2021
Pole positions:	20
First pole:	Doha 2021
Fastest laps:	6
Points:	1199
Titles:	MotoGP (2024), Moto3 (2018), Rookies Cup (2014)

2024 Season

Final position:	1st
Points:	508
Wins:	3

89
prima
PRAMAC
MOTUL

89

89
MARTINATOR
MICHELIN
alpinestars
PRAMAC
prima

89
prima
PRAMAC
LINO SONEGO
MOTUL

Franco Morbidelli

Prima Pramac Racing

Age:	29 (Born 4th December 1994)
Birthplace:	Rome (Italy)
Bike:	Ducati Desmosedici GP
Race number:	21
GPs started:	122
First GP:	Qatar 2018
Wins:	3
First win:	San Marino 2020
Pole positions:	2
First pole:	Catalunya 2020
Fastest laps:	1
Points:	687
Titles:	Moto2 (2017), Superstock 600 (2013)

2024 Season

Final position:	9th
Points:	173
Wins:	-

PRAMAC
prima
MOTUL
21
LINO SONEGO
WRS
FIAMM

prima
21
PRAMAC
MOTUL
FIAMM
WRS
LINO SONEGO

21

PRAMAC

PRAMAC
prima
MOTUL
21
WRS
LINO SONEGO
FIAMM
MICHELIN
DUCATI

Marc Márquez

Gresini Racing MotoGP

Age:	31 (Born 17th February 1993)
Birthplace:	Cervera (Spain)
Bike:	Ducati Desmosedici GP
Race number:	93
GPs started:	189
First GP:	Qatar 2013
Wins:	62
First win:	Americas 2013
Pole positions:	66
First pole:	Americas 2013
Fastest laps:	63
Points:	3018
Titles:	MotoGP (2013, 2014, 2016, 2017, 2018, 2019), Moto2 (2012), 125cc (2010)

2024 Season

Final position:	3rd
Points:	392
Wins:	3

DUCATI

SHOEI
Kapriol
Unibat
BOLD

93

Red Bull
FEDERAL OIL
Estrella Galicia
DUCATI

alpinestars
Allianz

Team Gresini Racing MotoGP

ALEX

Alex Márquez

Gresini Racing MotoGP

Age:	28 (Born 23rd April 1996)
Birthplace:	Cervera (Spain)
Bike:	Ducati Desmosedici GP
Race number:	73
GPs started:	89
First GP:	Spain 2020
Wins:	-
First win:	-
Pole positions:	1
First pole:	Argentina 2023
Fastest laps:	1
Points:	544
Titles:	Moto2 (2019), Moto3 (2014), CEV Moto3 (2012)

2024 Season

Final position:	8th
Points:	173
Wins:	-

MICHELIN
Unibat
Antangin
DUCATI

SHOEI
Red Bull
Kapriol
Antangin
Estrella Galicia
Unibat
BOLD

73

SHOEI
OLI
Estrella Galicia
ASPIRA
POLO CLUB

Antangin
Red Bull
OLI
MICHELIN
DUCATI

Marco Bezzecchi

Pertamina Enduro VR46 MotoGP Team

Age:	26 (Born 12th November 1998)
Birthplace:	Rimini (Italy)
Bike:	Desmosedici GP
Race number:	72
GPs started:	60
First GP:	Qatar 2022
Wins:	3
First win:	Argentina 2023
Pole positions:	4
First pole:	Thailand 2022
Fastest laps:	4
Points:	593
Titles:	CIV Moto3 (2015)

2024 Season

Final position:	12th
Points:	153
Wins:	-

72
ebay
HERO
PERTAMINA

ebay
PERTAMINA
Enduro
VR46

72

agv
ebay
72
HERO
PERTAMINA
PERTAMINA
Enduro

72
ebay
Enduro

Fabio Di Giannantonio

Pertamina Enduro VR46 MotoGP Team

Age:	26 (Born 10th October 1998)
Birthplace:	Rome (Italy)
Bike:	Ducati Desmosedici GP
Race number:	49
GPs started:	57
First GP:	Qatar 2022
Wins:	1
First win:	Qatar 2023
Pole positions:	1
First pole:	Italy 2022
Fastest laps:	1
Points:	340
Titles:	-

2024 Season

Final position:	10th
Points:	165
Wins:	-

SHOEI
monitor
CUPRA
ebay
49
PERTAMINA

Enduro
VR46
ebay
DUCATI

49

SHOEI
Enduro
ebay
monitor
CUPRA
49
HERO
PERTAMINA

MICHELIN

WDW2024
WORLDDUCATIWEEK
26th - 28th July / Misano, Italy
wdw.ducati.com

Lenovo Race of Champions

Alex Márquez

Álvaro Bautista

Andrea Iannone

Danilo Petrucci

Enea Bastianini

Fabio Di Giannantonio

Francesco Bagnaia

Franco Morbidelli

Glenn Irwin

Jorge Martín

Marc Márquez

Marco Bezzecchi

Michael Ruben Rinaldi

Michele Pirro

Nicolò Bulega

Step on board

Lenovo
NetApp
prima
Enduro
ebay
VARGROUP
aruba.it
TIM
23
89
21
72
49
93
73

Lenovo
NetApp
URBAN VISION

DUCATI

Lenovo
NetApp
MONSTER ENERGY
PARMACOTTO

Aruba.it Racing Ducati Team Presentation

22 January 2024
Madonna di Campiglio,
Trentino | Italy

2024 FIM Superbike World Championship Calendar

1 Australian Round
2 Catalunya Round
3 Dutch Round
4 Emilia-Romagna Round
5 UK Round
6 Czech Round
7 Portuguese Round
8 French Round
9 Italian Round
10 Aragón Round
11 Estoril Round
12 Spanish Round

aruba.it
MONSTER ENERGY
Lenovo
riello ups
FIAMM
CARRERA
SATECH
Modular Machine Guards
PANIGALE V4 R
Dierre
DUCATI

23-25 February | Australia

Australian Round

Phillip Island Grand Prix Circuit

Race 1	1. **Bulega (Ducati)** 2. Locatelli (Yamaha) 3. **Iannone (Ducati)**
Superpole Race	1. Lowes (Kawasaki) 2. Locatelli (Yamaha) 3. Razgatlioglu (BMW)
Race 2	1. Lowes (Kawasaki) 2. **Bautista (Ducati)** 3. **Petrucci (Ducati)**

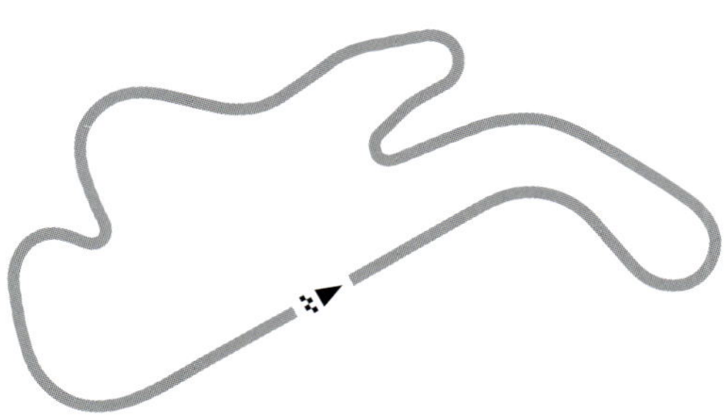

Circuit Record	Bulega (Ducati) 1m27.916s (182.015 km/h) - 2024
Fastest Lap	Bulega (Ducati) 1m28.564s (180.683 km/h) - 2024
Track Length	4.445 km
Corners	12 (7 left, 5 right)
Race Distance	1 x 20 laps (88.900 km), 1 x 10 laps (44.450 km), 1 x 11 laps (48.895 km)

Step on board

aruba.it
RACING
Ducati Superbike Team
DUCATI
CORSE
aruba.it
MONSTER
ENERGY
Lenovo
11

1
aruba.it
FIAMM
CARRERA
riello ups
Lenovo

54
ROKiT
11
aruba.it
FIAMM
Lenovo
29
HERO

GRAND PRIX CIRCUIT
ND RIDGE B

22-24 March | Spain

Catalunya Round

Circuit de Barcelona-Catalunya

Race 1	1. Razgatlioglu (BMW) 2. Bulega (Ducati) 3. Bautista (Ducati)
Superpole Race	1. Razgatlioglu (BMW) 2. Iannone (Ducati) 3. Bautista (Ducati)
Race 2	1. Bautista (Ducati) 2. Bulega (Ducati) 3. Razgatlioglu (BMW)

Circuit Record	Razgatlioglu (BMW) 1m39.489s (168.513 km/h) - 2024
Fastest Lap	Bulega (Ducati) 1m40.955s (166.066 km/h) - 2024
Track Length	4.657 km
Corners	14 (6 left, 8 right)
Race Distance	2 x 20 laps (93.140 km), 1 x 10 laps (46.570 km)

Step on board

Circuit de
Barcelona
PIRELLI
aruba.it
CARRERA
Lenovo

DIABLO
PIRELLI

aruba.it
Lenovo
STULZ
FIAMM
MONSTER

celona
MOTUL
ACTIONBOX
22
23
ENG
WorldSBK.com

3 | 12

19-21 April | Netherlands

Dutch Round

TT Assen Circuit

Race 1	1. Spinelli (Ducati) 2. Razgatlioglu (BMW) 3. Bautista (Ducati)
Superpole Race	1. Bautista (Ducati) 2. Bulega (Ducati) 3. Lowes (Kawasaki)
Race 2	1. Razgatlioglu (BMW) 2. Bautista (Ducati) 3. Gardner (Yamaha)

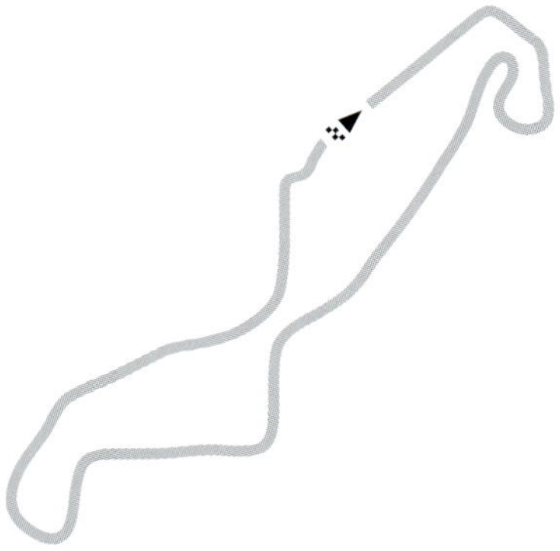

Circuit Record	Razgatlioglu (Yamaha) 1m32.934s (175.944 km/h) - 2022
Fastest Lap	Bautista (Ducati) 1m33.620s (174.655 km/h) - 2022
Track Length	4.542 km
Corners	18 (6 left, 12 right)
Race Distance	1 x 14 laps (65.762 km), 1 x 10 laps (45.420 km), 1 x 21 laps (95.382 km)

Step on board

24
dto

KYT
DUCATI
DAINESE
PIRELLI
nesite
FIAMM
CARRERA
aruba.it
MONSTER ENERGY
Lenovo
riello ups

Lenovo
Lenovo
55
87

4 | 12

14-16 June | Italy

Emilia-Romagna Round

Misano World Circuit
Marco Simoncelli

Race 1
1. Razgatlioglu (BMW)
2. **Bulega (Ducati)**
3. **Bautista (Ducati)**

Superpole Race
1. Razgatlioglu (BMW)
2. **Bulega (Ducati)**
3. Lowes (Kawasaki)

Race 2
1. Razgatlioglu (BMW)
2. **Bulega (Ducati)**
3. **Bautista (Ducati)**

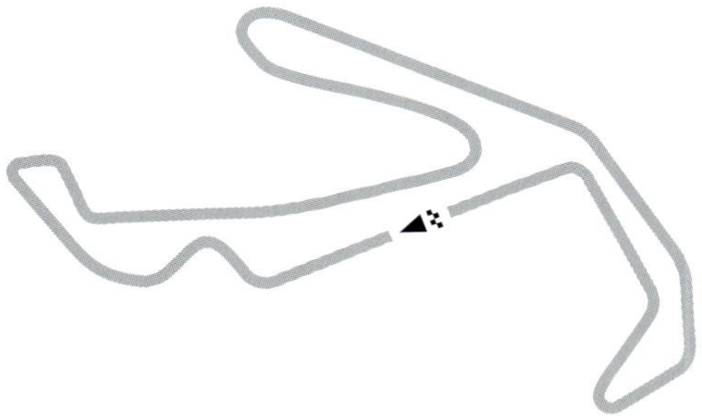

Circuit Record	Razgatlioglu (BMW) 1m32.320s (164.792 km/h) - 2024
Fastest Lap	Bautista (Ducati) 1m32.687s (164.140 km/h) - 2024
Track Length	4.226 km
Corners	16 (6 left, 10 right)
Race Distance	1 x 10 laps (42.260 km), 2 x 21 laps (88.746 km)

Step on board

TISSOT
TISSOT

aruba.it
RACING
Ducati Superbike Team
DUCATI CORSE
Lenovo
FIAMM
STULZ
11

aruba.it
RACING
MONSTER
CARRERA
motorola

aruba.it
51
11
Lenovo

aruba.it
STULZ
Lenovo
riello ups
FIAMM
MONSTER

aruba.it

12-14 July | Britain

UK Round

Donington Park

Race 1
1. Razgatlioglu (BMW)
2. Lowes (Kawasaki)
3. **Bautista (Ducati)**

Superpole Race
1. Razgatlioglu (BMW)
2. **Bulega (Ducati)**
3. Rea (Yamaha)

Race 2
1. Razgatlioglu (BMW)
2. **Bulega (Ducati)**
3. Lowes (Kawasaki)

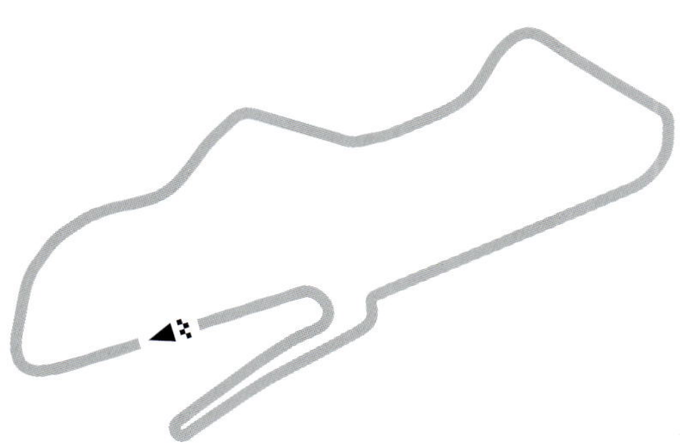

Circuit Record	Razgatlioglu (BMW) 1m24.629s (171.133 km/h) - 2024
Fastest Lap	Razgatlioglu (BMW) 1m25.597s (169.198 km/h) - 2024
Track Length	4.023 km
Corners	12 (5 left, 7 right)
Race Distance	1 x 10 laps (40.230 km), 2 x 23 laps (92.529 km)

Step on board

PROSECCO DOC
PROSECCO DOC
DODGE
DODGE
MOTUL

PIRELLI
MOTUL
MOTUL
MOTUL
DUCATI
aruba.it
Lenovo
AKRAPOVIC
MONSTER

MOTUL
ACTION BOX
aruba.it
Lenovo
riello ups

19-21 July | Czech Republic

Czech Round

Autodrom Most

Race 1

1. Razgatlioglu (BMW)
2. **Petrucci (Ducati)**
3. **Iannone (Ducati)**

Superpole Race

1. Razgatlioglu (BMW)
2. **Bulega (Ducati)**
3. Lowes (Kawasaki)

Race 2

1. Razgatlioglu (BMW)
2. **Bulega (Ducati)**
3. Locatelli (Yamaha)

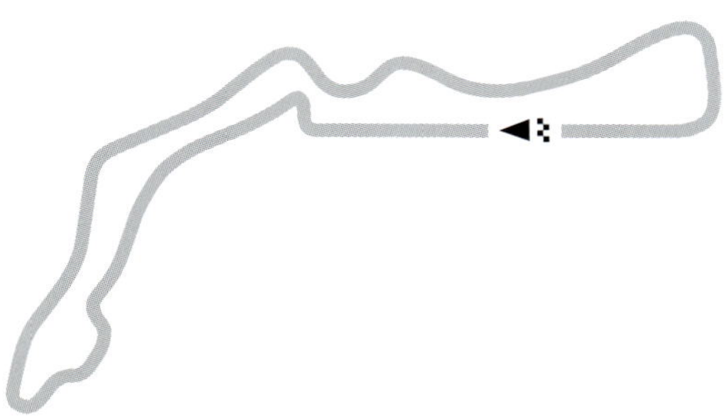

Circuit Record	Razgatlioglu (BMW) 1m30.064s (168.360 km/h) - 2024
Fastest Lap	Razgatlioglu (Yamaha) 1m31.180s (166.300 km/h) - 2022
Track Length	4.212 km
Corners	21 (9 left, 12 right)
Race Distance	1 x 10 laps (42.120 km), 2 x 22 laps (92.664 km)

Step on board

AUTODROM MOST
ACERBIS
PIRELLI
DIABLO
TISSOT
MOST AUTODROM

AUTODROM MOST
66
ADRIAN HUERTAS
ARUBA.IT RACING WORLDSSP TEAM
99
ALVARO BAUTISTA
ARUBA.IT RACING - DUCATI
1
aruba.it
Ducati Superbike Team
STULZ
Lenovo
riello ups
FIAMM
MONSTER ENERGY
DAINESE
ALTEN

DUCATI
motorola
ALTEN
DID
DAMAST
Motostorm

aruba.it
Lenovo

SBK

FIAMM
aruba.it
MONSTER
Lenovo
SBK
IM WORLD
PIONSHIP

7|12

9-11 August | Portugal

Portuguese Round

Autódromo Internacional do Algarve

Race 1	1. Razgatlioglu (BMW) **2. Bautista (Ducati)** **3. Petrucci (Ducati)**
Superpole Race	1. Razgatlioglu (BMW) **2. Petrucci (Ducati)** 3. Lowes (Kawasaki)
Race 2	1. Razgatlioglu (BMW) **2. Bulega (Ducati)** 3. Lowes (Kawasaki)

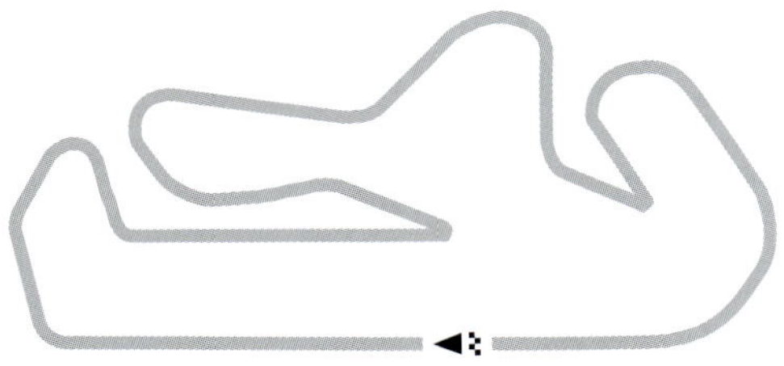

Circuit Record	Rea (Kawasaki) 1m31.610s (165.959 km/h) - 2022
Fastest Lap	Razgatlioglu (Yamaha) 1m39.826s (165.600 km/h) - 2023
Track Length	4.592 km
Corners	15 (6 left, 9 right)
Race Distance	1 x 10 laps (45.920 km), 2 x 20 laps (91.840 km)

Step on board

AIROH
REVIT
60
RGKIT

Lenovo
FIAMM
MONSTER

SBK
SUPERBIKE WOR
PIRELLI
IT's GENIO
itsgenio.com
SNACK
PATA
MAKE EX

8 | 12

6-8 September | France

French Round

Magny-Cours International Circuit

Race 1	1. Van der Mark (BMW)
	2. Bautista (Ducati)
	3. Petrucci (Ducati)
Superpole Race	**1. Bulega (Ducati)**
	2. Lowes (Kawasaki)
	3. Petrucci (Ducati)
Race 2	**1. Bulega (Ducati)**
	2. Petrucci (Ducati)
	3. Gerloff (BMW)

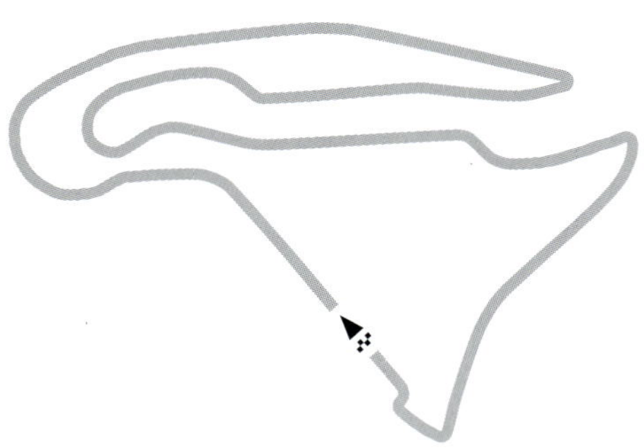

Circuit Record	Gerloff (BMW) 1m35.453s (166.360 km/h) - 2023
Fastest Lap	Bautista (Ducati) 1m36.084s (165.268 km/h) - 2023
Track Length	4.411 km
Corners	17 (8 left, 9 right)
Race Distance	1 x 10 laps (44.110 km), 2 x 21 laps (92.631 km)

Step on board

FIM
MOTUL
PIRELLI
aruba.it
FIAMM
CARRERA
DUCATI
nesite
MONSTER ENERGY
SBK
bonovo action
AKRAPOVIC
OUTDO
staykoala.com
OUTLETMOTO.EU

Lenovo
SATECH
Modular Machine Guards
PANIGALE V4 R
STULZ
aruba.it
DAINESE
ALTEN
11
PIRELLI
Lenovo
riello ups
FIAMM
UMANA
FERVI
D.I.D
NGK
AKRAPOVIC
MONSTER
ENERGY
DAMAST

aruba.it
Lenovo
riello ups
CARRERA
Pratiche
SBK

AIROH

9 | 12

20-22 September | Italy

Italian Round

Cremona Circuit

Race 1
1. Petrucci (Ducati)
2. Bulega (Ducati)
3. Bautista (Ducati)

Superpole Race
1. Petrucci (Ducati)
2. Lowes (Kawasaki)
3. Iannone (Ducati)

Race 2
1. Petrucci (Ducati)
2. Bautista (Ducati)
3. Bulega (Ducati)

Circuit Record	Bulega (Ducati) 1m27.953s (154.228 km/h) - 2024
Fastest Lap	Petrucci (Ducati) 1m28.289s (153.641 km/h) - 2024
Track Length	3.768 km
Corners	13 (7 left, 6 right)
Race Distance	1 x 10 laps (37.680 km), 1 x 17 laps (67.141 km) + 1 x 23 laps (86.664 km)

Step on board

DODGE
AIROH
BARDAHL

28
55
97
22
AIROH

NOLAN
SNACK
PATA
URBAN VISION
Lenovo
DELL'ORTO
29
HERO
VIGNALI
COMI
LOGISTICS

10 | 12

27-29 September | Spain

Aragón Round

MotorLand Aragón

Race 1	1. **Iannone (Ducati)** 2. Razgatlioglu (BMW) 3. Gerloff (BMW)
Superpole Race	1. **Bautista (Ducati)** 2. Lowes (Kawasaki) 3. **Bulega (Ducati)**
Race 2	1. **Bautista (Ducati)** 2. Razgatlioglu (BMW) 3. **Bulega (Ducati)**

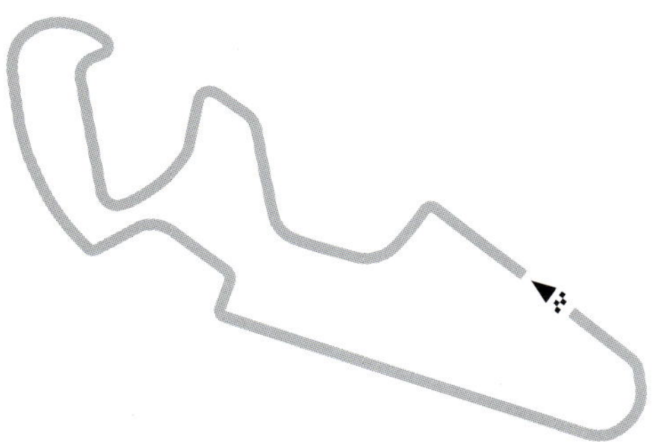

Circuit Record	Bulega (Ducati) 1m47.840s (169.484 km/h) - 2024
Fastest Lap	Razgatlioglu (BMW) 1m47.935s (169.335 km/h) - 2024
Track Length	5.077 km
Corners	17 (10 left, 7 right)
Race Distance	1 x 10 laps (50.770 km), 1 x 17 laps (86.309 km) + 1 x 18 laps (91.386 km)

Step on board

29
HERO
MAKE INNOVATION
DELLORTO
VIGNALI
logistic service provider
NILS
LAB
WRS
NOLAN
DITTA EDILE BALDINI CORRADO
DAINESE
URBAN VIS

DAINESE
PATA
SNACK
ELEVEN

aruba.it
Lenovo
CARRERA

TISSOT
TISSOT
MOTUL
MOTUL
PATA
URBAN VISION

STULZ
aruba.it
Lenovo
ALTEN

11 | 12

11-13 October | Portugal

Estoril Round

Circuito Estoril

Race 1	1. Razgatlioglu (BMW) **2. Bulega (Ducati)** 3. Lecuona (Honda)
Superpole Race	**1. Bulega (Ducati)** 2. Razgatlioglu (BMW) **3. Bautista (Ducati)**
Race 2	1. Razgatlioglu (BMW) **2. Bulega (Ducati)** **3. Bautista (Ducati)**

Circuit Record	Rea (Kawasaki) 1m35.346s (155.526 km/h) - 2022
Fastest Lap	Bulega (Ducati) 1m36.178s (156.535 km/h) - 2024
Track Length	4.182 km
Corners	13 (4 left, 9 right)
Race Distance	1 x 10 laps (41.820 km), 2 x 21 laps (87.822 km)

Step on board

aruba.it
Lenovo
CARRERA

aruba.it
DUCATI
Lenovo
FIAMM
CARRERA
MONSTER

aruba.it
Ducati Superbike Team
FIAMM
Lenovo
riello

aruba.it
Lenovo
ROKiT

12 | 12

18-20 October | Spain

Spanish Round

Circuito de Jerez – Ángel Nieto

Race 1	**1. Bulega (Ducati)** 2. Razgatlioglu (BMW) 3. Locatelli (Yamaha)
Superpole Race	**1. Bulega (Ducati)** 2. Razgatlioglu (BMW) 3. Lowes (Kawasaki)
Race 2	1. Razgatlioglu (BMW) **2. Bulega (Ducati)** 3. Van der Mark (BMW)

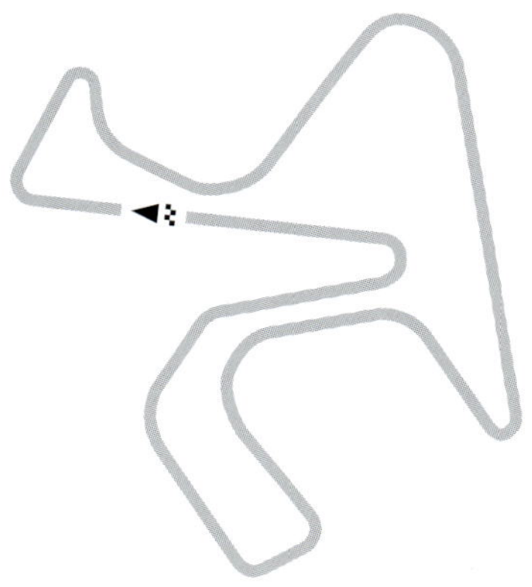

Circuit Record	Bulega (Ducati) 1m37.596s (163.150 km/h) - 2024
Fastest Lap	Bulega (Ducati) 1m38.528s (161.607 km/h) - 2024
Track Length	4.423 km
Corners	13 (5 left, 8 right)
Race Distance	1 x 10 laps (44.230 km), 1 x 20 laps (88.460 km) + 1 x 16 laps (72.988 km)

Step on board

SBK 2024
MANUFACTURERS' WORLD CHAMPION

PROMETEON

aruba.it
Lenovo

aruba.it
CARRERA
Lenovo
FIAMM

aruba.it
MOTUL

CIRCUITO DE
JEREZ
ÁNGEL NIETO
Ayuntamiento
de Jerez

Ducati Panigale V4 R Superbike

Motore / Engine	4 tempi, 4 cilindri a V di 90°, raffreddato a liquido, distribuzione desmodromica, 4 valvole per cilindro / 4-stroke, V4 90° liquid cooled, desmodromic distribution, 4 valves per cylinder
Cilindrata / Capacity	998 cc
Potenza / Power	> 235 CV @ 16000 giri/min all'albero / > 235 bhp @ 16,000 rpm at the crankshaft
Velocità massima / Maximum speed	> 315 km/h
Trasmissione / Transmission	Cambio a 6 marce con ingranaggi a denti dritti. Frizione STM con anti-saltellamento multidisco a secco con comando idraulico, trasmissione finale catena D.I.D / Six-speed gearbox with straight cut gears, dry multi-plate slipper clutch with hydraulic control, chain final drive
Gestione motore / Engine management	Magneti Marelli MLE | Centralina / Electronic Ignition-injection ECU
Alimentazione / Carburation	Iniezione elettronica, corpi farfallati motorizzati indipendenti a sezione ellittica / Electronic injection system, independent motorized elliptical throttle bodies
Iniettori / Injectors	Continental | Con farfalla aerodinamica, 2 iniettori per cilindro / With aerodynamic butterfly valves, twin injectors for each cylinder
Scarico / Exhaust	Akrapovič | 4 in 2 in titanio, 2 silenziatori in titanio / Titanium 4-2, with two titanium mufflers
Telaio / Chassis	Front frame in alluminio / Aluminium front frame
Sospensioni / Suspension	Öhlins | Forcella anteriore pressurizzata RVP2530 rovesciata da 46 mm. Forcellone monobraccio posteriore in alluminio con mono-ammortizzatore RVP50 / 46 mm pressurized RVP2530 upside-down fork, single-side aluminium swingarm, with RVP50 single shock absorber
Pneumatici / Tyres	Pirelli | Anteriori - 125/70-R17, posteriori - 200/65-R17 / Front 125/70-R17, rear 200/65-R17
Cerchi / Wheel rims	Marchesini | In lega di alluminio forgiato, disegno 5 razze a Y / Forged aluminium alloy, five-spoke Y design
Impianto frenante / Brakes	Brembo | Anteriore - Pinze monoblocco alettate in alluminio interamente ricavate dal pieno, con attacco radiale a 4 pistoni in titanio. Doppio disco freno in acciaio. Posteriore - Pinza in alluminio, con attacco assiale a 2 pistoni. Disco freno in acciaio / Front - Monobloc finned aluminium calipers entirely machined from solid, with a radial attachment of 4 pistons in titanium. Dual steel brake discs. Rear - Aluminium caliper with axial attachment of 2 pistons. Steel brake disc
Peso a secco / Dry weight	168 kg

aruba.it
Lenovo
riello ups
FIAMM
MONSTER ENERGY
SATECH
Modular Machine Guards
PANIGALE V4 R
DUCATI
Dierre
AKRAPOVIC
NGK
D.I.D
FERVI
motorola
DAMAST
flyme
PIEROBON

aruba.it
RACING
Ducati Superbike Team

aruba.it
RACING
aruba.it
RACING
Ducati Superbike Team
DUCATI
CORSE

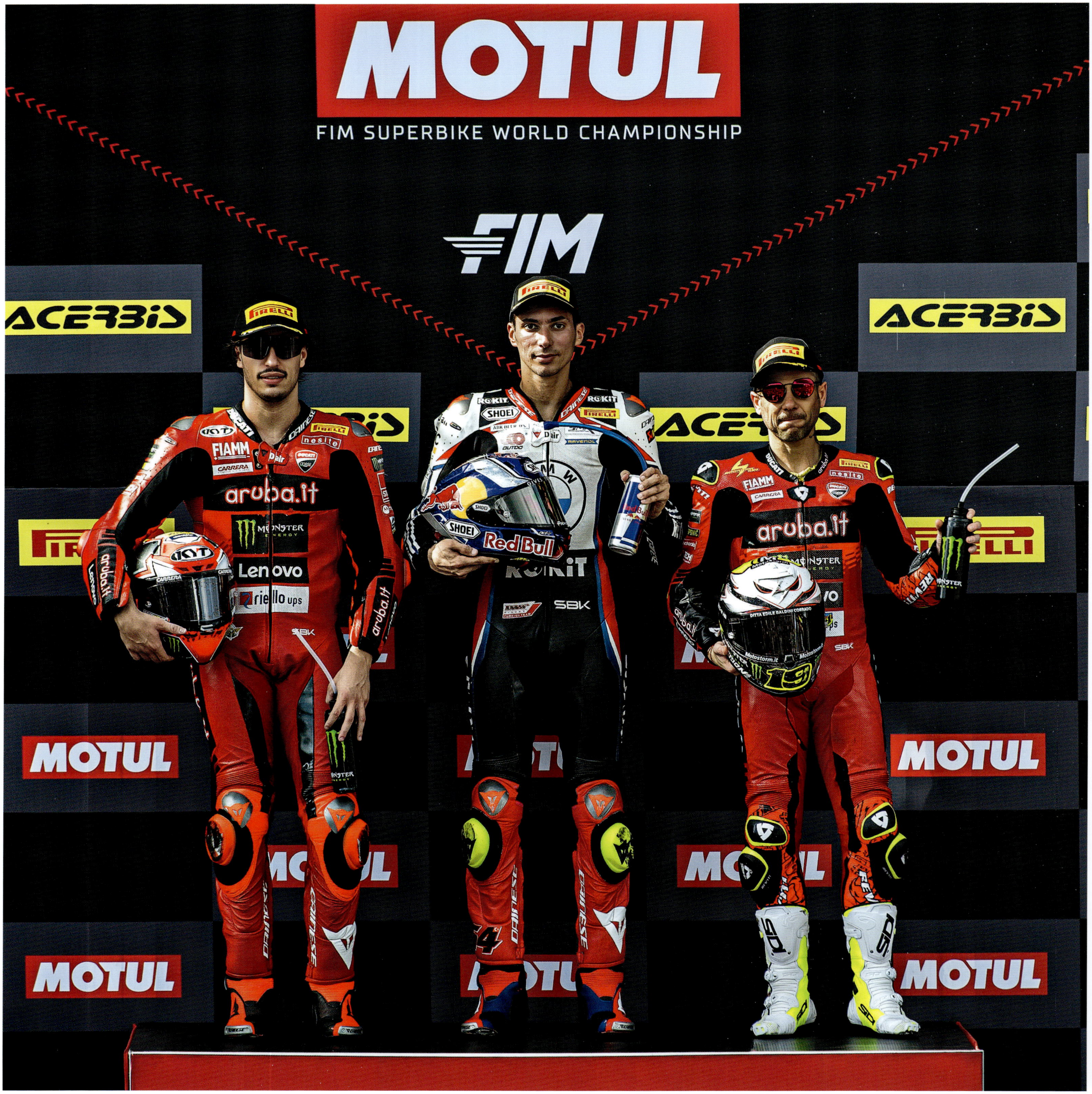
MOTUL
FIM SUPERBIKE WORLD CHAMPIONSHIP
FIM
ACERBIS
MOTUL

2024 SBK World Championship Classification

Position	Number	Rider	Nationality	Team	Points
1	54	Toprak Razgatlioglu	TUR	ROKiT BMW Motorrad WorldSBK Team	527
2	11	Nicolò Bulega	ITA	Aruba.it Racing – Ducati	484
3	1	Álvaro Bautista	ESP	Aruba.it Racing – Ducati	357
4	22	Alex Lowes	GBR	Kawasaki Racing Team WorldSBK	316
5	9	Danilo Petrucci	ITA	Barni Spark Racing Team	307
6	60	Michael van der Mark	NED	ROKIT BMW Motorrad WorldSBK Team	245
7	55	Andrea Locatelli	ITA	Pata Prometeon Yamaha	232
8	29	Andrea Iannone	ITA	Team GoEleven	231
9	31	Garrett Gerloff	USA	Bonovo Action BMW	176
10	87	Remy Gardner	AUS	GYTR GRT Yamaha WorldSBK Team	140
11	97	Xavi Vierge	ESP	Team HRC	137
12	7	Iker Lecuona	ESP	Team HRC	134
13	65	Jonathan Rea	GBR	Pata Prometeon Yamaha	127
14	47	Axel Bassani	ITA	Kawasaki Racing Team WorldSBK	108
15	45	Scott Redding	GBR	Bonovo Action BMW	107
16	77	Dominique Aegerter	SUI	GYTR GRT Yamaha WorldSBK Team	91
17	21	Michael Ruben Rinaldi	ITA	Team Motocorsa Racing	78
18	14	Sam Lowes	GBR	ELF Marc VDS Racing Team	53
19	24	Nicholas Spinelli	ITA	Barni Spark Racing Team	25
20	53	Tito Rabat	ESP	Kawasaki Puccetti Racing	22

Manufacturers

Position	Manufacturer	Points
1	Ducati	644
2	BMW	606
3	Kawasaki	339
4	Yamaha	307
5	Honda	185

Teams

Position	Team	Points
1	Aruba.it Racing – Ducati	841
2	ROKiT BMW Motorrad WorldSBK Team	775
3	Kawasaki Racing Team WorldSBK	424
4	Pata Prometeon Yamaha	359
5	Barni Spark Racing Team	332
6	Bonovo Action BMW	283
7	Team HRC	271
8	GYTR GRT Yamaha WorldSBK Team	240
9	Team GoEleven	231
10	Team Motocorsa Racing	78

aruba.it RACING
Ducati Superbike Team

BAUT1STA

Álvaro Bautista

Aruba.it Racing – Ducati

Age:	40
Birthplace:	Talavera de la Reina (Spain)
Bike:	Ducati Panigale V4 R
Race number:	1
Races Started:	204
First Race:	Phillip Island 2019
Wins:	63
First win:	Phillip Island 2019
Pole positions:	9
First pole:	Buriram 2019
Fastest laps:	56
Points:	2392
Titles:	2 x WorldSBK (2022 + 2023), 125cc (2006), CEV 125 (2003)

2024 Season

Final position:	3rd
Points:	357
Wins:	4

aruba.it
Lenovo
riello ups
flyme
motorola

PIRELLI
DUCATI
nesite
FIAMM
CARRERA
SBK
MOTUL

aruba.it
RACING
FIAMM
CARRERA
nesite
aruba.it
enovo

aruba
Lenovo

aruba.it RACING Ducati Superbike Team

BULEGA

Nicolò Bulega

Aruba.it Racing – Ducati

Age:	25
Birthplace:	Montecchio Emilia (Italy)
Bike:	Ducati Panigale V4 R
Race number:	11
Races Started:	36
First Race:	Phillip Island 2024
Wins:	6
First win:	Phillip Island 2024
Pole positions:	4
First pole:	Phillip Island 2024
Fastest laps:	11
Points:	484
Titles:	1 x WorldSSP (2023), CEV Moto3 (2015)

2024 Season

Final position:	2nd
Points:	484
Wins:	6

PIRELLI
DIABLO
PIRELLI

PIRELLI
DUCATI
FIAMM
CARRERA
aruba.it
MONSTER ENERGY
Lenovo
riello ups
SBK

11

aruba.it
Lenovo
riello ups
FIAMM
MONSTER
11

Lenovo
riello ups
FIAMM
MONSTER
11

Danilo Petrucci

Barni Spark Racing Team

Age:	34
Birthplace:	Terni (Italy)
Bike:	Ducati Panigale V4 R
Race number:	9
Races Started:	69
First Race:	Phillip Island 2023
Wins:	3
First win:	Cremona 2024
Pole positions:	-
First pole:	-
Fastest laps:	1
Points:	535
Titles:	CIV Superstock 2011

2024 Season

Final position:	5th
Points:	307
Wins:	3

AIROH
barni
RACING TEAM
REVIT!
DUCATI
dto
SPARK
PIRELLI
K9 BARDAHL

XCITEMENT
PIRELLI
REVIT!
AIROH
barni
RACING TEAM
SPARK
DUCATI
SBK
9
SBK MOTUL

AIROH
BARDAHL
dto
9
DUCATI
SPIDER
SBK

AIROH
BARDAHL
dto
9
SPIDER

Andrea Iannone

Team GO Eleven

Age:	35
Birthplace:	Vasto (Italy)
Bike:	Ducati Panigale V4 R
Race number:	29
Races Started:	36
First Race:	Phillip Island 2024
Wins:	1
First win:	MotorLand 2024
Pole positions:	-
First pole:	-
Fastest laps:	2
Points:	231
Titles:	-

2024 Season

Final position:	8th
Points:	231
Wins:	1

29

Michael Ruben Rinaldi

Motocorsa Racing

Age:	28
Birthplace:	Rimini (Italy)
Bike:	Ducati Panigale V4 R
Race number:	21
Races Started:	222
First Race:	MotorLand 2018
Wins:	5
First win:	MotorLand 2020
Pole positions:	-
First pole:	-
Fastest laps:	4
Points:	1289
Titles:	Superstock 1000 2017, CISP 125 2011

2024 Season

Final position:	17th
Points:	78
Wins:	-

DUCATI
PVM
brenta
TERENGHI
MOTOCORSA

BORGO
alpinestars
PIRELLI
PRO UP
STM

PVM
brenta
PRO UP
MOTOCORSA
Keller Zabby

BORGO
alpinestars
PIRELLI
TERENGHI
RAPPRESENTANZE ALIMENTARI
LS2 HELMETS
PRO UP 20g
STM

LOWES14

Sam Lowes

ELF Marc VDS Racing Team

Age:	34
Birthplace:	Lincoln (UK)
Bike:	Ducati Panigale V4 R
Race number:	14
Races Started:	30
First Race:	Phillip Island 2024
Wins:	-
First win:	-
Pole positions:	-
First pole:	-
Fastest laps:	1
Points:	53
Titles:	WorldSSP 2013, GB SS 2010

2024 Season

Final position:	18th
Points:	53
Wins:	-

14

PIRRO

Michele Pirro

Aruba.it Racing - Ducati
Barni Spark Racing Team (CIV)

Age:	38
Birthplace:	San Giovanni Rotondo (Italy)
Bike:	Ducati Panigale V4 R
Race number:	51
Races Started	12
First Race:	Magny-Cours 2013
Wins:	-
First win:	-
Pole positions:	-
First pole:	-
Fastest laps:	-
Points:	58
Titles:	7 x CIV SBK, 1 x CIV SSP, 2 x CIV STK, 1 x Euro 125

2024 Season

Final position:	25th
Points:	3
Wins:	-

DUCATI
FIAMM
MACNA
CARRERA
BforB

DUNLOP
PATA
ARLAM
BARDAHL
barni
RACINGTEAM
DUCATI
Unibat

51

DUCATI
CARRERA
aruba.it
51
Lenovo
riello ups

ARLAM
DUCATI
51
BARDAHL
GARAGES

2024 FIM World Supersport Championship

Final Standings

1	**Adrián Huertas (ESP)** Aruba.it Racing WorldSSP Team Ducati (#99)	439
2	**Stefano Manzi (ITA)** Pata Yamaha Ten Kate Racing (#62)	415
3	**Yari Montella (ITA)** Barni Spark Racing Team Ducati (#55)	382
4	**Valentin Debise (FRA)** Evan Bros. World SSP Yamaha Team (#53)	238
5	**Marcel Schroetter (GER)** MV Agusta Reparto Corse (#23)	228
6	**Jorge Navarro (ESP)** Orelac Racing Verdnatura Ducati (#9)	192
7	**Federico Caricasulo (ITA)** Motozoo ME Air Racing MV Agusta (#64)	184
8	**Glenn van Straalen (NED)** Pata Yamaha Ten Kate Racing (#28)	165
9	**Lucas Mahias (FRA)** GMT94 Yamaha (#94)	155
10	**Thomas Booth-Amos (GBR)** PTR Triumph (#69)	120

Manufacturers

1	**Ducati**	556
2	Yamaha	474
3	MV Agusta	293
4	Triumph	181
5	Kawasaki	99
6	Honda	29

MOTUL
HONDA

EICMA
99
55
28

55
99
aicox
DUCATI

WORLD CHAMPION
DUCATI

2024 British Superbike Championship

Calendar

1 **19-21 April**
Circuito de Navarro (SPA)

2 **4-6 May**
Oulton Park

3 **17-19 May**
Donington Park

4 **14-16 June**
Knockhill

5 **5-7 July**
Snetterton

6 **19-21 July**
Brands Hatch

7 **9-11 August**
Thruxton

8 **24-26 August**
Cadwell Park

9 **13-15 September**
Oulton Park

10 **27-29 September**
Donington Park

11 **11-13 October**
Brands Hatch

Final Standings

1	**Kyle Ryde** OMG GRILLA Yamaha Racing (#77)	487
2	**Tommy Bridewell** Honda Racing UK (#1)	486
3	**Glenn Irwin** Hager PBM Ducati (#2)	382
4	**Danny Kent** McAMS Racing Yamaha (#52)	373
5	**Ryan Vickers** OMG GRILLA Yamaha Racing (#7)	349
6	**Christian Iddon** Oxford Products Racing Ducati (#21)	261
7	**Lee Jackson** MasterMac Honda (#14)	251
8	**Josh Brookes** FHO Racing BMW (#25)	249
9	**Leon Haslam** ROKiT Haslam Racing BMW (#91)	228
10	**Andrew Irwin** Honda Racing UK (#18)	226

hager
Silkolene
hager
hager

hager
Silkolene
BRIGGS
DUCATI

21
OXFORD
OXFORD

hager
hager

2024 MotoAmerica Superbike Championship

Calendar

1 19-21 April
Michelin Raceway Road Atlanta, GA

2 17-19 May
Barber Motorsports Park, AL

3 31 May-2 June
Road America, WI

4 14-16 June
Brainerd International Raceway, MN

5 28-30 June
Ridge Motorsports Park, WA

6 12-14 July
WeatherTech Raceway Laguna Seca, CA

7 16-18 August
Mid-Ohio Sports Car Course, OH

8 13-15 September
Circuit of The Americas, TX

9 27-29 September
New Jersey Motorsports Park, NJ

Final Standings

1	Josh Herrin Warhorse HSBK Racing Ducati (#2)	350
2	Cameron Beaubier Tytlers Cycle Racing BMW (#6)	280
3	Bobby Fong Wrench Motorcycles Yamaha (#50)	253
4	Sean Dylan Kelly TopPro Racing BMW (#40)	226
5	Loris Baz Warhorse HSBK Racing Ducati (#76)	224
6	Cameron Petersen Attack Performance Yamaha (#45)	215
7	Jake Gagne Attack Performance Yamaha (#1)	192
8	JD Beach Tytlers Cycle Racing BMW (#95)	151
9	Brandon Paasch Vision Wheel M4 ECSTAR Suzuki (#96)	115
10	Ashton Yates Jones Honda (#27)	98

LAP
TIME
LAP
FERRACCI
OnlyFans
DUCATI
DUNLOP

2024 MotoAmerica Supersport Championship

Calendar

1 **19-21 April**
Michelin Raceway Road Atlanta, GA

2 **17-19 May**
Barber Motorsports Park, AL

3 **31 May-2 June**
Road America, WI

4 **14-16 June**
Brainerd International Raceway, MN

5 **28-30 June**
Ridge Motorsports Park, WA

6 **12-14 July**
WeatherTech Raceway Laguna Seca, CA

7 **16-18 August**
Mid-Ohio Sports Car Course, OH

8 **13-15 September**
Circuit of The Americas, TX

9 **27-29 September**
New Jersey Motorsports Park, NJ

Final Standings

1	**Mathew Scholtz** Strack Racing Yamaha (#11)	360
2	**PJ Jacobsen** Rahal Ducati Moto (#15)	331
3	**Blake Davis** N2 Racing Yamaha (#22)	212
4	**Jake Lewis** Altus Motorsports Suzuki (#85)	202
5	**Tyler Scott** Vision Wheel M4 ECSTAR Suzuki (#70)	194
6	**Corey Alexander** Rahal Ducati Moto (#23)	176

Daytona 200

1 **Josh Herrin**
Warhorse HSBK Racing Ducati (#2)

2 **Tyler Scott**
Vision Wheel M4 ECSTAR Suzuki (#70)

3 **Hayden Gillam**
Vesrah Racing Suzuki (#95)

4 **Richie Escalante**
Vision Wheel M4 ECSTAR Suzuki (#54)

5 **Karel Hanika**
YART ProKASRO Yamaha (#98)

6 **Marvin Fritz**
YART ProKASRO Yamaha (#17)

DAYTONA
200

DUNLOP

2024 CIV Italian Superbike Championship

Calendar

1 **6-7 April**
Misano World Circuit Marco Simoncelli
Misano Adriatico, Emilia-Romagna

2 **25-26 May**
Autodromo Vallelunga Piero Taruffi
Campagnano di Roma, Lazio

3 **22-23 June**
Autodromo Internazionale del Mugello
Scarperia, Tuscany

4 **3-4 August**
Misano World Circuit Marco Simoncelli
Misano Adriatico, Emilia-Romagna

5 **31 August - 1 September**
Autodromo Internazionale del Mugello
Scarperia, Tuscany

6 **28-29 September**
Autodromo Internazionale Enzo e Dino Ferrari
Imola, Emilia-Romagna

Final Standings

1	Michele Pirro Barni Spark Racing Team Ducati (#51)	238
2	Alessandro Delbianco DMR Racing Yamaha (#52)	197
3	Samuele Cavalieri Nuova M2 Racing Aprilia (#76)	172
4	Luca Bernardi Nuova M2 Racing Aprilia (#19)	161
5	Riccardo Russo DMR Racing Yamaha (#84)	121
6	Simone Saltarelli TCF Racing Team Honda (#73)	115
7	Luca Vitali Scuderia Improve Honda (#70)	101
8	Lorenzo Gabellini SLP Corse BMW (#36)	90
9	Gianluca Sconza SLP Corse BMW (#53)	59
10	Roberto Mercandelli Broncos Racing Team Ducati (#93)	49

mugello
CIRCUIT

AKRAPOVIC
BARDAHL
barni
RACING TEAM
DUCATI

CIV
barni
RACING TEAM
DUCATI
dto
BARDAHL

2024 EWC Endurance World Championship

Calendar

1 **24H Motos, 20 April**
Circuit Bugatti, Le Mans (France)

2 **8 Hours of Spa Motos, 8 June**
Circuit de Spa-Francorchamps (Belgium)

3 **Suzuka 8 Hours, 21 July**
Suzuka Circuit, Suzuka (Japan)

4 **Bol D'Or, 14 September**
Circuit Paul Ricard, Le Castellet (France)

2024 MFJ Superbike All Japan Championship

Calendar

1 **10 March**
Suzuka International Circuit

2 **13-14 April**
Mobility Resort Motegi

3 **25-26 May**
Sports Land Sugo

4 **16 June**
Tsukuba

5 **25 August**
Mobility Resort Motegi

6 **7-8 September**
Autopolis

7 **29 September**
Okayama International Circuit

8 **26-27 October**
Suzuka International Circuit

Final Standings

1	**Yuki Okamoto** Yamaha Factory Racing Team (#2)	230
2	**Katsuyuki Nakasuga** Yamaha Factory Racing Team (#1)	211
3	**Ryo Mizuno** Ducati Team Kagayama (#3)	209
4	**Kohta Nozane** Astemo HondaDream SI Racing (#32)	150
5	**Takumi Takahashi** JAPAN POST HondaDream TP (#33)	121
6	**Teppei Nagoe** SDG Honda Racing (#4)	89

DUCATI CORSE
DUCATI
MOTUL
SDG

DUCATI
3
32

2024 FIM MotoE World Championship

Calendar

1 Autódromo Internacional do Algarve (Portugal)

2 Le Mans (France)

3 Circuit de Barcelona-Catalunya (Spain)

4 Autodromo Internazionale del Mugello (Italy)

5 TT Circuit Assen (Netherlands)

6 Sachsenring (Germany)

7 Red Bull Ring - Spielberg (Austria)

8 Misano World Circuit Marco Simoncelli (Italy)

Final Standings

	Rider / Team	Points
1	**Héctor Garzó (SPA)** Dynavolta Intact GP MotoE (#4)	246
2	**Mattia Casadei (ITA)** LCR E-Team (#40)	231
3	**Óscar Gutiérrez (SPA)** Axxis-MSI (#99)	208
4	**Kevin Zannoni (ITA)** Openbank Aspar Team (#21)	191
5	**Alessandro Zaccone (ITA)** Tech3 E-Racing (#61)	179
6	**Jordi Torres (SPA)** Openbank Aspar Team (#81)	152
7	**Nicholas Spinelli (ITA)** Tech3 E-Racing (#29)	149
8	**Matteo Ferrari (ITA)** Felo Gresini MotoE (#11)	132
9	**Andrea Mantovani (ITA)** KLINT Forward Factory Team (#9)	113
10	**Eric Granado (BRA)** LCR E-Team (#51	112

AIROH
4
enel
moto e
ODYSSEY

40
Oleo-Mac
enel
Castrol
Arai

69
DUCATI
enel
LAGOM GROUP

DUCATI
Openbank
21
solunion
enel

2024 Italian Prestige Motocross Championship – MX1

Calendar

1	16-17 March Mantova, Lombardy
2	20-21 April Cingoli, Marche
3	25-26 May Montevarchi, Tuscany
4	22-23 June Ponte a Egola, Tuscany
5	31 August-1 September Castiglione del Lago, Umbria
6	12-13 October Pietramurata, Trentino

Final Standings

1	Alessandro Lupino (Ducati)	2174
2	Jan Pancar (KTM)	1946
3	Giuseppe Tropepe (Honda)	1431
4	Alvin Östlund (Honda)	1400
5	Andrea Bonacorsi (Yamaha)	1370
6	Isak Gifting (Yamaha)	1168
7	Cédric Soubeyras (Kawasaki)	1135
8	Filippo Zonta (KTM)	858
9	Simone Croci (Honda)	784
10	Stefano Pezzuto (Yamaha/Honda)	771

DUCATI

THOR
GALFER
SHOWA
PIRELLI
VARGROUP
AIROH

AIROH
DUCATI
POLIZIA

DUCATI
MONSTER

Ringraziamo per la preziosa collaborazione nella realizzazione del libro / We wish to thank the following for their invaluable collaboration in the preparation of this book:

Editor-in-Chief: **Julian Thomas**

Project Management: **Francesca Rossetti, Elisa Guberti**

Art Direction: **Elisa Guberti**

Photography Supervisor: **Sandro Pavoni**

Layout and Photolithography: **Silvana Editoriale S.p.A.**

Cover Photo: **Jesus Robledo**

Principal Photography: **Alex Farinelli (MotoGP), Matteo Cavadini/ Alex Photo (SBK)**

Contributing Photographers: **Jesus Robledo, Alejandro Ceresuela, Manuelo Bececco, Matteo Vernasca, Gabriele Galli, Matteo Lepri, Rodrigo Merino González, Marco Rimondi, Bonnie Lane (BSB), Brian J. Nelson (MotoAmerica), Matteo Lepri (CIV), Aki Kusudo (EWC / Japan SBK), Davide Messora / Daniele Barreca (MX1)**

Post-Production Supervisor: **Miguel Hernández**

Post-Production Cover Photo: **Giulio Pedaci - Ritoccando**

Post-Production: **Alt®ALuce S.r.l.**

Consultants: **Yuri De Cassan, Artur Vilalta, Julie Giovanola**

Ringraziamo il Dorna Sports per le foto studio dei piloti MotoGP, le foto MotoE e Dorna WSBK Organization per le foto studio dei piloti WSBK / Thanks to Dorna Sports for the use of the studio photos of the MotoGP and the MotoE images, and Dorna WSBK Organization for the studio photos of WSBK riders.

Direzione / Management: Claudio Domenicali, Luigi Dall'Igna, Mauro Grassilli, Davide Tardozzi, Stefano Cecconi, Daniele Casolari, Serafino Foti, Paolo Ciabatti.

Squadre / Teams: Ducati Lenovo Team, Prima Pramac Racing, Gresini Racing MotoGP, Pertamina Enduro VR46 Racing Team, Aruba.it Racing - Ducati, Barni Spark Racing, Team GO Eleven, MotoCorsa Racing, ELF Marc VDS Racing Team, Aruba.it Racing WorldSSP Team, Orelac Racing, Hager PBM Ducati, Oxford Products Racing Ducati, Warhorse HSBK Racing Ducati, Rahal Ducati Moto, Broncos Racing Team, Ducati Team Kagayama, Ducati Factory MX Team.

Piloti / Riders: Francesco Bagnaia, Enea Bastianini, Jorge Martín, Franco Morbidelli, Marc Márquez, Alex Márquez, Marco Bezzecchi, Fabio Di Giannantonio, Álvaro Bautista, Nicolò Bulega, Danilo Petrucci, Andrea Iannone, Sam Lowes, Michael Ruben Rinaldi, Michele Pirro, Adrián Huertas, Yari Montella, Glenn Irwin, Christian Iddon, Josh Herrin, Loris Baz, PJ Jacobsen, Ryo Mizuno, Alessandro Lupino, Antonio Cairoli, tutti gli altri piloti Ducati, lo staff Ducati Corse e i nostri tifosi / all the other Ducati riders, Ducati Corse staff and our fans.

General Director: **Michele Pizzi**

Editorial Director: **Sergio Di Stefano**

Editorial Coordinator: **Laura A. Maggioni**

Cover Design: **Giacomo Merli**

Layout: **Claudia Brambilla**

Press Office: **Alessandra Olivari, press@silvanaeditoriale.it**

Finito di stampare nel mese di novembre 2024 /
Printed in November 2024

Stampato in Italia / Printed in Italy:
Tipo Stampa, Moncalieri (Torino)

ISBN: 978-88-366-5865-7

FSC
www.fsc.org
MIX
Paper | Supporting responsible forestry
FSC® C150257